Hope and Despair in the American City

Hope and Despair

in the American City
Why there are
no bad schools
in Raleigh

Gerald Grant

Harvard University Press
Cambridge, Massachusetts
London, England

First Harvard University Press paperback edition, 2011

Library of Congress Cataloging-in-Publication Data

Grant, Gerald.
Hope and despair in the American city :
why there are no bad schools in Raleigh / Gerald Grant.
p. cm.
Includes bibliographical references and index.
ISBN 978-0-674-03294-1 (cloth: alk. paper)
ISBN 978-0-674-06026-5 (pbk.)
1. School improvement programs—North Carolina—Raleigh—Case studies.
2. Urban schools—United States—Case studies.
3. Urban renewal—United States—Case studies.   I. Title.
LB2822.83.N8G73   2009
371.009173′2--dc22   2008050594

To my children, Robert Grant, Katharine Stryker, and Sarah Bliss, each of whom, in different ways, is an inspiring teacher

Contents

Hope and Despair in the American City

Introduction

This is a book about the triumph of hope over despair in an American city—about how the lives of children in one metropolitan area have been transformed in ways that reduce racism and break the yoke of poverty. It is about Raleigh, North Carolina, a city of robust growth where more than eight out of ten students pass state tests in reading and mathematics.

But this is also the sadder story of Syracuse, New York, which has suffered the decline characteristic of most urban centers in America—a city whose school system is overwhelmed by the poverty and racial isolation of the children it serves, and where fewer than three out of ten eighth graders pass state tests in reading and math. In order to spread the hope that Raleigh symbolizes, we need to understand how that city overcame the despair that plagues so much of urban America today. We must explain how citizens voluntarily tore down the invisible wall that kept inner-city children out of Raleigh's affluent suburban schools. In the 1960s and 1970s, barriers like the one in Raleigh—composed of exclusive zoning regulations, discriminatory public housing policies, and misbegotten court decisions—were erected in metropolitan areas throughout the nation to separate black from white, rich from poor, with devastating consequences for children on the wrong side of the wall.

Aware of these life-altering disparities in educational opportunity, some writers have demonized those who choose to live in the suburbs as being indifferent to the fate of cities, if not outright racist. But I believe most people's motives are more complicated than that, and so I begin this tale of two cities with my own move to the suburbs in 1972.

My wife, Judy, grew up in Manhattan, and I was born in Syracuse, where I graduated from Central High School. After marriage we lived in Washington, D.C., in a fourth-floor walk-up on 17th Street near Dupont Circle and then bought a row house on 28th Street a few blocks from the zoo. Our three children were born in Washington. We thought of ourselves as cosmopolitan urbanites and would have answered "Over my dead body" if a poll similar to one conducted in New York City had asked D.C. residents whether they would move to the suburbs, given an opportunity. (In New York, 29 percent checked that choice.)

We saw the suburbs as bland, sterile Levittowns, or as pretentious subdivisions that would gradually sprout McMansions— places without a sense of history or soul that were destroying the rural landscape and befouling the air with endless commuting. We did not want to spend half our lives in a car on clogged highways during rush hour, or shuttling children from home to a distant shopping mall to church to music lessons. In 1968, while I was a graduate student, we moved to Brookline, Massachusetts, a densely populated but affluent town with electric streetcars, just over the line from Boston. Our children attended a racially integrated elementary school within walking distance of our home.

By the time I became a professor at Syracuse University in 1972, all our children were in grade school. We decided to

2

choose a school first and a house second. We began our search in city neighborhoods near the university. But in school after school, we felt we were being processed by a bureaucracy rather than welcomed as future parents. Worse, especially for my wife —a progressive educator who had founded the Lowell School in Washington, which placed a high value on the arts and creative play—the schools we visited were dispiriting. In the one we liked best, all the pictures lining the hallway were nearly identical turkeys that the children had colored inside the lines. Judy's classroom visits confirmed her feeling that the teaching was as stilted and unimaginative as the turkeys.

The next day she saw an ad for a house in a charming village bordering the north end of Skaneateles, one of the most beautiful of the Finger Lakes. Real estate was still reasonably priced in those days, though by the time President Bill Clinton and his family spent a summer vacation there while Hillary campaigned for the U.S Senate, lake properties were selling for a million or more. We bought a house a thousand yards from the lakefront, where I swam every day until the October chill set in. We were invited to join the village country club, but since neither of us were golfers, we declined. We did take sailing lessons there with our children and occasionally played tennis with friends.

At this point in her life, Judy was content to put her career aside for a while to be a stay-at-home mom. In addition to volunteering at the local nursing home, she ran the Cub Scout pack, joined the town Democratic Committee, and enjoyed the special pleasures of village life, where the children could walk safely to school and bike to the town center a half-dozen blocks away. We met interesting neighbors, including a couple down the street who gave our children pottery lessons in the garage they had converted to a studio. Our daughter raised pigeons in the small barn behind our house. We walked to our children's track meets and field hockey games and took our dogs to cider-making parties and barbecues. At the July 4th celebration, the whole town turned out to watch the band and the Boy Scouts march past. That night, we all went down to the lake to enjoy the fireworks. Lanterns hanging on docks formed a shimmering ring of light on the water. We slipped easily into the life of suburbanites, fixing up our old house and tending our yard and garden. We found Skaneateles anything but sterile.

There were only two elementary schools in town, on opposite ends of a huge campuslike setting with the middle school and high school in the center. The difference between entering Waterman Elementary, which our children attended, and some of the city schools we had visited was like the difference between going to a friend's house for coffee and standing in line at a welfare office. Skaneateles teachers dressed and acted like professionals. The gymnasiums, art facilities, and science labs were outstanding. The well-equipped playing fields stretching for acres over carefully clipped grass reminded me of a visit to the lush campus of St. Paul's boarding school in New Hampshire.

It occurred to me much later that parents like us were really buying quasi-private schooling for our children. With the exception of a few farming families at the outer reaches of the town, Waterman Elementary was for upper-middle-class families who could afford to buy Skaneateles properties and pay the high real estate taxes that funded its educational system. These parents felt as though they owned their schools, and they got the kind of treatment from educators and staff that parents expect from a good private academy. Many of them were fed up with the bureaucratic rigidity of the urban school systems they had left. They sought schools that were not heavily unionized and were responsive to their needs. Parents were willing to pay higher salaries for teachers who had gone to good colleges and universities, and they expected those teachers to write convincing letters of recommendation so that their children would be admitted to institutions of the same caliber.

What parents seemed not to expect was diversity. They (we) were all white. Even elite schools like St. Paul's made a point of admitting a handful of low-income black students on scholarship. There were no black children in Skaneateles.

Without a doubt, some parents had moved to the town for that very reason. They wanted to escape the urban crime and vulgar behavior they associated with mostly black neighborhoods in the city. Some of them were outright racists. But most residents of Skaneateles seemed to be motivated by factors having little to do with race. Many were attracted to the suburbs by the considerable tax advantages of federally insured mortgages. In his classic book on suburban migration, Kenneth Jackson estimated that federal subsidy for middle- and upper-middle-class homeowners in the form of mortgage and tax benefits was several times the subsidy for welfare families in the inner city.[1] But perhaps the strongest motives were the dream of owning one's piece of the American rural landscape and the promise of upward mobility. Particularly for millions of immigrants, the move out of urban ghettos into the suburbs, to a spacious lot with a two-car garage, was the sign of having made it. As a bonus, you got to associate with others who had made it, who were the comers, the successful entrepreneurs, the managerial class whose business and professional associations could be of direct benefit to you and your children.

I was not untouched by these motivations myself. My wife came from an old New York family and was the third generation to attend college. Her grandfather, chairman of the Bowery Savings Bank, graduated from City College, but the next two generations went to Princeton and Vassar. While Judy worked hard as a student and educator, she didn't worry so much about "making it." I had a different story.

My grandfather was a Scots-Irish immigrant who died in his forties, leaving a family of five children. My late father had quit school after eighth grade to work in a butcher shop and later in a Syracuse steel mill to support his family. On hot summer nights, my brother and I would pile into the backseat of his old Packard, and he would drive us from our modest home on the south side of Syracuse to Skaneateles, where we took a dip in the lake near the bandstand of the town park, hoping not to be noticed. My mother had grown up in the Eastern Star Orphanage in Rome, New York, and I knew she would be proud to see her professor son owning a home in upscale Skaneateles. I made a point of taking her to the grand Sherwood Inn for lunch and then walking her across the street to watch our children swim in the lake, which by that time had signs posted "Residents Only."

We had been living in Skaneateles for six years when I invited a former high school teacher and mentor to dinner. A photograph of us standing on the front porch shows me with a beard, striped purple shirt, and purple bell-bottom pants. Judy wore a miniskirt. That picture brings to mind the day my daughter came home from school after some hazing by her classmates, asking in a hurt voice, "Daddy, are we hippies?" I guess we were, in a way. My former teacher had risen to become assistant superintendent of personnel for the Syracuse City School District. At the end of dinner, he offered Judy a job teaching fourth grade at the Martin Luther King Elementary School.

It was not an easy decision for us. The school district's policy required new employees to live in the city, although we learned afterward that the rule was rarely enforced and was abolished altogether a few years later. But we reasoned that our bucolic time in Skaneateles had given our children a good start in life, and I was tiring of the eighteen-mile commute. A visionary African-American high school classmate of mine was principal of the King School and drawing excellent teachers who wanted it to succeed as a community school serving some of the neediest black children in the city. Both Judy and I had been volunteering in a Catholic soup kitchen in Syracuse that served dinner to more than a hundred homeless people every Sunday. Judy was eager to make the commitment that was being asked of her and return to teaching.

The more we talked, the more excited we became about this new adventure. We wanted our children to have the experience of living in an urban neighborhood and attending public schools with a diverse student body. We decided to cancel a planned sabbatical in Italy, and during the summer of 1978 we moved to Syracuse. Judy began teaching at Martin Luther King Elementary that fall.

1 | What Happened to America's Cities?

W̲e̲ were elated to be back in the city. We had first looked at houses in Berkeley Park, a white upper-middle-class faculty enclave close to the university campus but decided to buy further east in the Westcott neighborhood, one of the most diverse census tracts in the city. Locals referred to it as Westcott Nation, a tribe of independent artists, writers, gays, students, blacks, whites, Asians, Hispanics, and disabled persons living in group homes. A middle-class African-American family lived on one side of us, an artist from Puerto Rico on the other. Orthodox Jews in wide-brimmed hats walked to their synagogue on Saturday mornings, while political activists stapled protest signs on telephone poles in the business district. Westcott was economically as well as racially diverse. Poor families lived in an extensive housing project at the north end of the neighborhood, professors and other professionals lived in spacious homes a few blocks south, and a large number of working-class and middle-class families were sandwiched in between.

Westcott's location seemed to meet our needs perfectly. Judy and I could have a dinner party and then drive to Symphony Hall or Syracuse Stage in five minutes. I enjoyed the walk to my campus office, overlooking the city from the hills in Thornden Park. This was the same park where, in 1981, Alice Sebold, a Syracuse undergraduate, would be raped—a brutal attack described twenty years later in her brilliant memoir *Lucky*.

The first chill in our urban euphoria came during a party one night when a bunch of young hooligans ran up on our side porch, yelling and pounding on the French doors and startling our wine-sipping guests on the other side. I ignored them at first, but when they came back a few minutes later I took off after them while my wife called the police. When a young officer arrived, he listened politely to my tale and then lectured me for giving chase, saying this was what the teenagers wanted—to get a rise out of me. "What did you expect, living in this neighborhood?" Shocked, I asked him where he lived, and he said Camillus, one of the suburbs. "What if this happened to your wife while she was alone in the kitchen? Would you be happy to hear that a Camillus police officer told her what you just told me?" He sheepishly agreed that he wouldn't.

What I did not realize then was that this young policeman was no anomaly. He represented the enormous abandonment of the city by its police, teachers, and firemen. Police officers no longer felt that the city was a safe place to raise a family. When I was growing up on the south side, several of my teachers lived in our neighborhood and nearly all of them lived in the city, as did our firemen and police. By the late twentieth century these civic servants rarely resided in the city. In a recent visit to the Syracuse high school where my son graduated in 1985, the principal could think of only three teachers out of a faculty of 120 whose own children attended city schools.

Because of our volunteering experiences in the soup kitchen, Judy and I already had some idea of the city's decline. But I did not realize the extent of it until I began to take bike rides around my old neighborhood and elsewhere, and saw acres of boarded-up and abandoned housing. The 1960s and 1970s were the decades of heaviest flight, and by the end of the century Syracuse had lost nearly 40 percent of its population. A city of 220,000 in 1950 had shrunk to 139,000 by 2008.

At the end of World War II, Syracuse was still a boomtown with a mixed industrial base. Nearly 80 percent of the real property value was in the city, with little more than a fifth of taxable land in the suburbs of Onondaga County. Willis Carrier founded what became the largest air-conditioning company in the world on the west side of the city. Learbury clothing made suits for Brooks Brothers (you could buy them at the factory for half price) and many other brandname companies—Nettleton Shoes, New Process Gear (which made parts for General Motors cars), General Electric, Will and Baumer Candles, and the Solvay Process Company (later Allied Chemical)—prospered here. Syracuse University quadrupled in size under the GI Bill.

It was a city with marked ethnic neighborhoods: Irish on Tipperary Hill, and Italians, Poles, and Germans clustered in heavily Catholic parishes on the north side. The city's Protestant manufacturing elites lived in the Sedgwick area off James Street on the east side or the Strathmore area circling the green hills of Onondaga Park. Many Jews still lived in what locals then unselfconsciously referred to as Jewtown, the old area of Jewish bakeries and kosher meat shops just southeast of downtown. It abutted the black settlement referred to as the Fifteenth Ward—or, among some whites, Niggertown. Joyce Carol Oates, who was an undergraduate at Syracuse, captured both the sociological context and the ethnic politics of the city in her novel *What I Lived For.*[1]

Syracuse Central High School, an impressive neoclassical building designed by Archimedes Russell, stood on the edge of the Fifteenth Ward. In 1955, the year I graduated, Central High enrolled Jews and blacks, working-class students from my neighborhood on the south side, as well as the children of Carrier executives who lived in Strathmore. The mayor's son was a member of my class. Some parents moved from rural parts of the county so that their children could attend a school where Latin, Greek, French, Russian, German, and Spanish were taught. Although blacks graduated at a much lower rate than whites, the school served a racial, ethnic, and economic cross-section of the city. It was a model of the American common school ideal, open to all comers.

Even before World War II, middle-class and professional Jewish families began to spread out of the old Jewish neighborhood into the Westcott area and even further, into new homes being built on the hills of the city's east side. An Orthodox temple, a Jewish community center, and a large funeral home that mostly served Jews were built in Westcott, as well as a bakery selling bagels and horn rolls. Supported by New York's fair-employment legislation and expanding job opportunities, some African Americans moved into housing abandoned by Jews and fanned out slowly block by block. But discriminatory housing practices confined most blacks to the Fifteenth Ward. School district lines were gerrymandered and primarily black public elementary schools were enlarged to ensure that African Americans stayed within the ward's slightly expanded contours.[2]

Most of the Fifteenth was demolished in the 1960s, as major infusions of state and federal funds underwrote a grand policy of "slum clearance." This urban renewal project was linked with plans for interstate highway construction that would cut through and destroy many old city neighborhoods, white as well as black. But only the Fifteenth Ward was virtually bulldozed out of existence. After the ground was prepared for the two interstate highways that would intersect downtown, the heart of the city looked as though it had been strip-mined. Whites began to leave the city in droves, including people in my old neighborhood of Brighton. Some whites who left were undeniably motivated by racism, but others simply did not want to live near noisy, ugly interstate highways that chopped up their backyards.

The "renewal" plan included a major cultural complex of museums and parks adjacent to a new government center. To some eyes, the futuristic city hall designed by Paul Rudolph resembled an airport in a Third World country more than a monumental government office building in the United States. Aside from the stunning Everson Museum of Art designed by I. M. Pei and a new civic center, most of the complex, including the sprawling city hall, was never built. What Syracuse got was wider highways on concrete stilts that slashed through the heart of downtown and destroyed its most historic buildings. A handful of new high-rise apartments, surrounded by parking lots, towered starkly over the interstate highway.

The state and federal government had found money to tear up downtown and construct new roads, but not much to build anything new, except for public housing. And that is what Syracuse, like many other cities, proceeded to do. One of the largest of the new public housing tracts, named Rolling Green Estates, stretched for several blocks along the northern border of the Westcott area. In 1950 nine African Americans lived in that census tract. By 1970, following a decade of urban renewal, 1,444 black residents lived there, most of them in Rolling Green Estates and most of them poor. During this period, the percentage of black residents rose from less than 1 percent to 40 percent, and the percentage of owner-occupied housing dropped from 48 to 25 percent, as more than half of white homeowners left the neighborhood. Many single-family homes were bought up by absentee landlords and converted to multiunit dwellings.[3]

Shunting the poorest blacks into massive housing projects like Rolling Green Estates not only isolated them from other working-class and middle-class African Americans with whom they had lived in the Fifteenth Ward but also set them apart from middle-class whites in their new neighborhood. Rolling Green residents were concentrated in a treeless, dense concrete-and-brick zone five blocks long, surrounded by a six-foot spiked black iron fence that stood in grim contrast with the frame housing, front yards, and gardens in the rest of Westcott. A few storefront churches opened along the perimeter of the project, but these hardly compensated for the massive loss of social networks experienced by the poor black children of Rolling Green. After the old mixed-class black settlement was destroyed, the proportion of single-parent black households increased, and Rolling Green was soon shrouded in an atmosphere of despair. Before long, some of the public housing built in that era was itself boarded up, abandoned by residents fearful of crime and drug wars.

Options other than clearance and removal of blacks were never seriously considered. A combination of historic preservation, rehabilitation, and upgrading of existing housing with voluntary scattered-site relocation of black residents could have maintained a real community with stores, churches, and neighborhood organizations while increasing the possibility for residential integration. Although segregated, the old Fifteenth Ward was a neighborhood that offered jobs, informal mentoring, and community support. All of those social structures were destroyed when the buildings were leveled.

What happened in Syracuse was hardly unique. It was repeated on a larger scale in Newark, Chicago, and St. Louis, where the demolition of the drug-ridden Pruitt-Igoe housing project in 1972 was considered by many to be a turning point in both American architecture and urban planning. The story of Syracuse is but a small part of a larger web of social policies and programs that shaped urban decline across the nation.

Redlining

When we moved to Syracuse we knew nothing of the devastating effects of federal redlining, which affected the mortgage-ability and insurance-worthiness of every neighborhood in America. The seven-bedroom house we bought had been built in 1921 by a prominent physician not long after a trolley line reached Westcott Street and opened that recently incorporated area of Syracuse to rapid development. It sat on a double corner lot with a two-car garage, an attached storage shed, and a large backyard which appealed to my gardener-wife. Having been well-maintained by its successive owners, our new house was, if anything, of superior construction to the house we had owned in Skaneateles. We had sold that house at a good price and were able to pay cash for the Westcott property, so I did not apply for a mortgage. Yet when I called the insurance agent who had insured our Skaneateles house as well as other properties throughout the county, I was told that our house in Westcott was not insurable. Astonished, I asked how that could be. We had never brought an insurance claim during our six years in Skaneateles, so we clearly were not a high risk. We had a good credit record and had made all our payments on time. I was baffled. My conversation with the agent went something like this:

Was the property overvalued? Did we pay too much for it?

No, I wouldn't say that. [Pause]

Well, what could possibly be the reason you won't insure a good customer?

Your house is in a redlined neighborhood.

What?

A redlined neighborhood. It's a rating system. It means the banks and insurance companies believe it's a bad risk.

We consulted our new neighbors and eventually found an insurance company that would write a policy for us. Later, after I became active in our neighborhood association, I learned more about redlining. When my parents bought their small house on the south side for $3,500 in 1927, mortgages were typically given for only five or ten years. During the 1920s building boom, mortgages that had not been paid off in five years were usually easily renewed. But when the Depression hit, the loans were called and many families lost their homes. In 1933 President Roosevelt acted to protect small homeowners from foreclosure by establishing the Home Owners Loan Corporation (HOLC) to refinance loans over a longer period with smaller payments—similar to today's thirty-year fixed-rate mortgage. In its first two years HOLC supplied more than a million mortgages, and about 40 percent of all eligible Americans sought HOLC assistance.

Yet as the Depression deepened, foreclosure rates remained high in some states, even with refinancing. To better predict the productive life of dwellings it financed and hence determine the degree of loan risk for its long-term mortgages, HOLC in 1937 developed color-coded maps based on systematized appraisals of virtually every neighborhood in America. The lowest or fourth-grade neighborhoods were outlined in red, hence "redlined." The older, more densely populated, and more ethnically or racially mixed a neighborhood was, the lower its rating. At the other end of the spectrum, first-grade housing, colored green, referred to new "homogeneous" neighborhoods "in demand as residential locations in good times and bad." These were homes owned by "American business and professional men," which often meant that real estate covenants prevented the sale of houses to Jews or minorities. Neighborhoods with an "infiltration of Jews" could not be considered first-grade.

When I had an opportunity to look at the maps, I saw that even in 1937 most of the Westcott neighborhood was coded blue, or second-rate, in part because Jews had begun to move in. Bluelining signaled to mortgage lenders that home loans should be capped at 10 to 15 percent below the maximum amount allowed for comparable homes in a green-coded neighborhood. One section of Westcott near a small commercial strip was coded yellow for "definitely declining," because of older multifamily buildings and properties where owners lived above their stores. The kind of mixed-use housing in commercial areas that Jane Jacobs celebrated in 1961—because it meant more "eyes on the street" and encouraged pedestrian-friendly environments that are the heart of urban life—was devalued by the HOLC appraisers in 1937.[4]

Berkeley Park, which had a covenant to protect buyers and was laid out in graciously curved streets with parkways dividing the traffic, was rated first-grade, as were other elite neighborhoods—Strathmore, Sedgwick Park, and Bradford Hills. The Fifteenth Ward, by contrast, was entirely redlined, although it housed only a minority of blacks at that time. HOLC appraisers, mostly real estate personnel, were told to redline a block even if only one black family resided there, on the assumption it would soon be all-black and "undesirable" or even "hazardous." HOLC gave greater weight to the socioeconomic characteristics of a neighborhood than to the structural condition of its housing. Even new homes occupied by blacks were coded red.

Of course HOLC did not invent the prejudices its codes reflected. Racism was widely ingrained in real estate sales throughout the United States. The codes that HOLC adapted had been earlier codified by the sociologists Homer Hoyt and Robert Park at the University of Chicago, who showed how the social status of residents was linked to property values. Hoyt was among the first to describe the illegal tactic of blockbusting, whereby developers or brokers would help a black person overpay for a house in a white neighborhood, and then incite fear among whites that the entire block would soon become black. When whites panicked and put their homes on the market at drastically reduced prices, the broker would buy up the property and sell it at a profit to other black families.

The tragedy of HOLC was not in creating its secret Residential Security Maps—they were not secret for very long—but in enshrining and giving government legitimacy to racism on an unprecedented scale. HOLC established a pattern of underfunding mortgages for older urban houses while providing easy access to mortgages in the suburbs—a practice that exploded after World War II. HOLC's maps were adopted by the Federal Housing Agency (FHA) and later were widely used by banks and other private lenders as well as insurance companies. The FHA, supplemented by a GI Bill that helped more than 16 million veterans purchase a home after World War II, did not make direct loans but insured other lenders who gave mortgages for properties that met FHA guidelines.

No other government program had more effect on the pattern of urban and suburban development than FHA. After the war, most of the nation's largest builders designed their new homes to meet the agency's standards, and banks followed its racist appraisal guidelines, modeled on the HOLC codes. In fact, FHA instructed appraisers to look first at the HOLC maps in order "to segregate for rejection many of the applications involving locations not suitable for amortized mortgages." Its guidelines stipulated that rigid white-black separation must be maintained: "If a neighborhood is to retain stability, it is necessary that properties shall continue to be occupied by the same social and racial classes."[5]

The FHA manuals praised neighborhoods with restrictive covenants that barred sales to "inharmonious racial or nationality groups." In one Detroit neighborhood where whites began to buy new homes near a black settlement, neither blacks nor whites could get FHA insurance because of the proximity of "inharmonious" racial groups. But after a clever white developer built a concrete wall between the white and black areas, the FHA appraisers returned and approved mortgages on the white properties. Although the United States Supreme Court struck down racial property covenants in 1948, the FHA did not change its guidelines on covenants until 1950. Its updated redlining maps continued to be used for decades by banks and insurance agents. They were still in effect when we moved to Syracuse in 1978.

While the racism embedded in FHA redlining unquestionably did the most damage to African Americans, the FHA's policies also dealt a crippling blow to the cause of historic preservation and renewal of America's cities. The agency gave the green light to the purchase of new housing on terms never before available to the average American. Before FHA, banks commonly granted mortgages for only 60 percent or less of a property's value, necessitating large down payments or credit-worthiness for second mortgages. The FHA, by contrast, required only 10 percent down and low monthly payments on thirty-year mortgages. This made buying a home cheaper than renting for most Americans. Its guidelines favored new single-family housing in all-white

18

subdivisions. Levittowns and other suburban developments boomed with what for developers was an FHA bonanza. Yet not one of Long Island's 82,000 Levittown residents was black in 1960. When asked about this policy, William Levitt said, "We can solve a housing problem, or we can try to solve a racial problem. But we cannot combine the two."[6]

FHA's policies assumed that cities would decline, and so they automatically downgraded older housing. Giving a second-grade rating to stable older urban neighborhoods with good-quality housing meant that a mortgage there would cost more than one in a new first-grade suburb. The redlining of Westcott in the 1970s, owing to the neighborhood's mixed commercial use, multiunit dwellings, and racial integration, meant that mortgages were often difficult to obtain without large down payments. Yet Westcott boasted some of the most architecturally distinguished residences in the city.

Metropolitan St. Louis illustrates this pattern as well as any American city. By 1960 the suburbs received five times as much FHA mortgage insurance as the city of St. Louis. The disparity in home improvement loans was nearly as great. Although the city had more aging housing, the suburbs received improvement loans amounting to three times the funds given to city properties. After the urban riots in the 1960s, Senator Paul Douglas of Illinois summed up for the National Commission on Urban Problems the damage FHA policies had done:

> The poor and those on the fringes of poverty have been almost completely excluded. These and the lower middle class, together constituting the 40 percent of the population whose housing needs are greatest, received only 11 percent of the FHA mortgages . . . Even middle-class residential districts in the central cities were suspect, since there was always the prospect that they, too, might

turn as Negroes and poor whites continued to pour into the cities, and as middle and upper-middle-income whites continued to move out.[7]

This led to the National Housing Act of 1968, which directed the FHA to soften its guidelines and direct more housing loans to blighted urban areas. Still the pattern of suburban dominance continued. By 1976 the St. Louis suburbs had received $1.1 billion in loans, while only $314 million went to the city. The blight in both St. Louis and Syracuse continued to spread. Historic housing built with the finest materials and close attention to architectural detail was allowed to rot under leaky roofs. A 2002 study of FHA loans found that less than 5 percent had gone to low-income areas in Syracuse and only 1.3 percent to predominantly minority areas.[8]

In the past decade, significant federal funds for home improvement have come into Westcott and other neighborhoods in Syracuse. Ironically, Congressman James Walsh, son of the mayor who had pushed for "slum clearance" in the Fifteenth Ward, steered these federal monies to Syracuse to repair some of the harm caused by misbegotten policies of urban renewal forty years earlier.

Suburban Separatism

One morning on my commute to work from Skaneateles in the mid-1970s, I turned on the radio to hear the deep voice of Syracuse's first black school superintendent, Sidney Johnson. It was a news bite reporting a speech he gave suggesting that Syracuse, with the cooperation of suburban school districts, ought to foster more racial integration by voluntary busing of black children who chose to go to suburban schools, even if on a small scale. It had been working in Boston and could work here, he believed. But the suburban school superintendents gave Johnson a cold shoulder. None picked up on his suggestion, and no city child was bused to a suburban public school.

Superintendent Johnson was right about the Boston experiment, however. The Metropolitan Council for Educational Opportunity (METCO) began busing black children to the Boston suburbs in 1966, nearly a decade before court-ordered busing began within the city's public schools. When Judy and I lived in the Boston suburb of Brookline in 1968–1972, the elementary school our children attended received METCO children. The program started in 1966 with 220 children being bused to seven suburbs, some of them quite affluent, and by 2008 approximately 3,130 students were traveling to 32 participating METCO communities. More than 15,000 were on waiting lists, with a quarter of the parents signing up their children before their first birthday. Over 8,000 children had graduated from high school under the METCO program, and 86 percent of them went on to college. While black parents who volunteered for the METCO experiment valued diversity, they ranked the suburban schools' academic excellence as the most important reason for participating.[9]

At the start, however, some blacks complained about the METCO experiment. They feared it would draw off the most talented students from city schools and lead to the erosion of African-American communities. The children would have to endure long bus rides to schools where they might not be welcome, and they might internalize the white racism of suburban schools, coming to despise their own origins. Some argued that the money should be used to improve black schools in the city. In

The Other Boston Busing Story, a remarkable study of black adults who as children attended suburban schools under the METCO program, Susan Eaton explored these and other claims.[10]

Eaton heard many stories of humiliation when METCO children got to the end of the bus line in the suburbs. Our house was on the Brookline side of the border with Boston, and our driveway was literally on the city line. The Edward Devotion Elementary School, which our children attended, received a busload of black children from Boston each day. On Parents' Visiting Day I went to classes with my daughter, then in second grade. At lunch I noticed that most of the blacks were sitting together. "It's too bad they don't yet feel comfortable sitting with the white students," I commented to the white children at my daughter's table. One of them replied sharply, "Nobody wants to sit with them, some of those niggers have knives." I held back a gasp and suggested perhaps the black children were angry because they had overheard white children calling them by such a hateful name. Then I did gasp when my own daughter spoke up: "But Daddy, some of those niggers do have knives." I rebuked her for using a word I had never heard from her before, and said maybe they feared her more than she feared them. I went on to try to help the white children understand how the black children might feel as strangers coming into a school where they had no friends and were shunned and humiliated by some resentful white children. I also suggested some positive steps they could take to help the black children feel more welcome.

The METCO students experienced plenty of pain, but in long interviews with Eaton they rarely focused on the negative. They said those feelings faded as they made friends and developed new social networks. And my own children benefited as well from the opportunity, as whites, to interact with black children in class and on the playground. One of my daughters and my son grew up to become teachers in integrated public schools, attributing their career choice in part to having acquired an ease in more diverse settings early in life. Some of the METCO teachers regarded discussion of race as taboo, but others opened conversations that helped lessen tensions. One of the many virtues of the program was that it provided counselors in Roxbury, where most of the black children lived, who could help students cope with the hostility they encountered. Cooperating suburbs also found a host family for each black child—most often a family whose own child was in the same classroom—so that children would have at least one home in the town where they could count on feeling welcome.

The black adults in Eaton's study said they did not lose their black identities but learned to bridge two worlds. Even those who moved to the suburbs as adults—about a third—maintained their connections with black communities through churches and social organizations. The payoff in social mobility far outweighed the costs of long bus rides and occasional hostile acts. More than 90 percent of the black adults in Eaton's sample said they would choose to get on a METCO bus again if they had to live their lives over. And many of these adults have enrolled their own children in the METCO program.

METCO children escaped from the limited information networks of the inner city. As adults, they attributed their success in getting into college and finding good jobs to what they learned by crossing lines of race and class. They made contacts with people who knew about better jobs and could get them interviews or write letters on their behalf. They gained confidence as they learned the codes and unwritten rules of the white middle-class world. They discovered how to express themselves as blacks in white settings, and they learned how to "talk with anyone about anything." They were more at ease in job interviews with whites, knowing how to "break the ice."[11]

In two major studies of Chicago's urban poor, the sociologist William Julius Wilson found that isolation from middle-class information networks and lack of social skills to negotiate across class lines were the greatest barriers to upward mobility. A study of more than 4,000 employers found that blacks who could draw on racially integrated social networks were in higher-paying positions, while those restricted to segregated networks were in the lowest-paid jobs in settings with few white co-workers.[12]

The decision of the Syracuse suburbs to turn their backs on a METCO-like experiment involving the daytime presence of a few black children in their schools was a tragedy. But an even greater tragedy was the resistance in Syracuse and many other cities to moves designed to open up suburban housing to the urban poor. Public housing projects that had been authorized under the New Deal were originally built as temporary housing for the working poor. But over time they became permanent housing for a black and Hispanic underclass, helping to create ever greater concentrations of urban poor. In Chicago, one huge federally funded housing project was nearly a mile wide and two miles deep. Suburbs across the Northeast could have applied for public housing funds for their own towns, yet almost none did.

In the late 1970s, Dorothy Gautreaux, a tenant activist in Chicago public housing, brought a class-action suit charging the Chicago Housing Authority (CHA) with setting policies that fostered extreme racial segregation among public housing applicants and residents. This was the first significant breach in a wall that kept most federal money for public housing in the cities. After years of litigation that went all the way to the Supreme Court, Gautreaux won. The courts ordered the Department of Housing and Urban Development (HUD) and the CHA to provide vouchers to 7,100 black families so that they could move to racially integrated or predominantly white neighborhoods. Under what became known as the Gautreaux program, nearly three quarters of residents with these Section 8 vouchers (named for Section 8 of the 1937 Housing Act) moved to predominantly white areas, most of them in suburbs. More than a decade later, researchers interviewed these suburban mothers to learn what had happened to them and their children, and compared these outcomes with those of mothers who used the vouchers to move their children out of the projects but not out of the city.

As was the case with the Boston METCO program, the children in the Gautreaux program who moved to the suburbs experienced some hostility. But they had lower dropout rates than those who stayed in urban neighborhoods, and they were more likely to take math and science courses in preparation for college. A significantly higher percentage of the suburban high school graduates went to four-year colleges, and more of them became employed full time as young adults.[13]

In the 1970s HUD Secretary George Romney tried to generate integrated, scattered-site housing projects in predominantly white neighborhoods, but the Nixon administration derailed those efforts. President Jimmy Carter began efforts to export the Gautreaux experiment to other parts of the country under the Regional Mobility program, but the Reagan administration terminated the program in 1981, calling it an inappropriate form of "social engineering."[14]

Syracuse, like most cities, used its limited number of Section 8 vouchers to direct applicants to city rental properties, often not far from the housing projects they were trying to escape. Regulations in some suburbs of Syracuse prohibited the use of Section 8 vouchers within their jurisdiction unless the holder of the voucher had been a resident of the suburb for at least a year. This Catch-22 meant in effect that poor or working-class residents of some suburbs could qualify for Section 8 vouchers, but a black resident of the city could not use the same federal subsidy to cross the city line in search of better housing. Owners of vacant city housing, many of whom lived in the suburbs, also brought political pressure to have Section 8 tenants directed to their urban properties rather than to the suburbs. It was not until the late 1990s that the courts struck down these suburban regulations. Yet as late as 2008, when dilapidated public housing was torn down in Syracuse, new units were rebuilt on the same site instead of in the suburbs. In short, federal and state housing funds continue to be awarded primarily to replicate existing concentrations of the urban poor.[15]

In 1994, under the Clinton administration, a second major federal experiment was launched in the suburbs to open housing to the urban poor. Called Moving to Opportunity, it began on a small scale, like the Gautreaux program, by funding vouchers in five cities that enabled residents of public housing to move to the suburbs. Within only a few years, after opposition arose in the suburbs of Baltimore, a major expansion of this program was crushed by Congress, where a majority of the votes were cast by members who had been elected in suburban America. However, research on the results of the first stage of the experiment continued. More than half of those who applied for the MTO program said the major reason they wanted to move was fear of crime, drugs, and gang violence in the projects. Many felt like prisoners in their own homes, afraid to leave at night to attend a parents' meeting at school or to allow their children to venture into the streets. The second most popular reason was a desire for better schools for their children.[16]

Results varied among the five cities, but the overwhelming finding in all cities was that MTO residents who moved to the suburbs felt a new freedom from fear. The researchers also found that children achieved more in school, at least in some cities. But the MTO experiment went beyond Gautreaux to collect data on jobs, health, and crime. Jobs as well as housing opportunities were at the heart of the MTO program. A pattern found in Syracuse was common to most urban areas: major plants such as General Electric and Carrier Air Conditioning had moved from the city to the suburbs to find cheap land where the huge one-story buildings necessary for assembly-line production could be constructed. Not only had concentrations of poverty grown in the city but work had disappeared to the suburbs, as Wilson showed in his study of Chicago. The MTO program made it possible for residents of housing projects to move where the jobs were.

In Boston, voucher holders found jobs and better training opportunities in the suburbs than those available to them in the inner city, and welfare rates for MTO recipients dropped by half, while overall health improved markedly. Among children with asthma in Boston, the number of attacks over a six-month period fell dramatically. Those who moved to the suburbs reported they were less tense and suffered less depression compared with a control group who remained in city housing projects. Within a year after moving to the suburbs, the arrest rate of teenage boys in these families fell significantly, perhaps because they were less subject to coercion by gang members. They experienced fewer behavioral problems in school, and more of the suburban girls, who now felt safe outside their homes, reported having at least one close friend.[17]

Fair Share Housing

The Moving to Opportunity program was a sizable social experiment involving 4,608 families, and by 2000 it had helped pave the way for an expansion of Section 8 housing vouchers to subsidize rents for more than two million low-income families. But it was only a small crack in the wall that had been built to exclude the urban poor from the suburbs. Throughout most of the nineteenth century, annexation of surrounding towns and villages was common: state legislatures granted strong annexation powers to cities, and surrounding communities benefited from city water, sewers, policing, and fire protection. A turning point came in 1874 when Brookline, calling itself the "richest town in the world," voted against consolidation with Boston. Wealthy and independent suburbs across the nation followed suit. Oak Park and Evanston rejected annexation by Chicago; Brighton and Irondequoit spurned Rochester. Proposed consolidations failed in St. Paul in 1924 and in Cleveland in 1925.

These affluent suburbs wanted control of their social and physical environment. A suburban Chicago weekly editorialist wrote: "The real issue is not taxes, nor water, nor street cars—it is a much greater question than either. It is the moral control of our village . . . Under local government we can absolutely control every objectionable thing that may try to enter our limits—but once annexed we are at the mercy of the city hall." As the immigrant population increased in the early part of the twentieth century, the view from the periphery shifted. Immigrants were now seen as supporting corrupt city government and were stereotyped as the root causes of crime, drunkenness, and urban disorder.[18]

Villages and suburbs moved preemptively to incorporate in order to prevent takeovers, and the boundaries between cities and suburbs hardened. The ring of suburbs around cities like Detroit and St. Louis became more stratified by income and social class. Real estate agents touted the superior benefits of suburban schools, and even Ralph Waldo Emerson used schools to lure new residents to his beloved Concord: "We will make our schools such that no family which has a new home to choose can fail to be attracted hither as to the one town in which the best education can be secured." Whereas strong annexation laws had been based on the principle that sharing resources provided the greatest good for the greatest number, by the mid-twentieth century many states adopted regulations that protected the independence of suburbs. In 1967, Staten Island even threatened to secede from New York City.

Seventy percent of the nation's population lived in 193 cities in 1950, but half a century later the total population had almost doubled and the situation was nearly the reverse, with more than 60 percent living in suburbs. Cities in states granting annexation powers were able to capture this suburban growth and enlarge their tax base. They unified fragmented governments, created strong regional identities, and shared the wealth. But in other states, city-suburban boundaries remained frozen and metropolitan governments balkanized. Even in states where annexation was permitted, many of the most populous cities were complacent. Already wealthy and dominant in their regions as the era of suburban expansion dawned, they focused on controlling what they had and dividing the pie rather than on making it bigger.[19]

In Syracuse, for example, a 1953 proposal to strengthen countywide government was overwhelmingly defeated by a vote of 3 to 2, with the highest negative votes in the suburban towns and villages. The fragmented government in the metropolitan area led to "insoluble deadlocks" that frequently blocked ac-

29

tion. When the position of county executive was finally created, some functions—notably sewage and water—were taken over by the county government. But this was done on an ad hoc basis without achieving any real change in the inequalities between city and suburbs. While the adoption of a county sales tax led to some tax sharing, no regional planning to provide scattered-site housing for the poor or preservation of green space was adopted.[20]

A different pattern prevailed in many states that permitted annexation, especially in the South and West. Dallas grew from a medium-sized city of 45 square miles in 1940 to one of 350 square miles in 1960. The average Texas city grew tenfold. Oklahoma City annexed vast tracts of land. City-county consolidations occurred in Nashville (with Davidson County in 1963), Indianapolis (with Marion County in 1970), and Lexington, Kentucky (with Fayette County in 1973). Jacksonville, Florida, united with Duval County in 1968, and by 1980 it had grown to 841 square miles, becoming the largest city in the continental United States.[21]

Cities that expanded their boundaries often adopted planning and zoning policies that helped spread affordable housing across the region. They were more likely to have integrated schools, where income and racial disparities were markedly reduced. On a segregation index where a score of 100 indicates complete apartheid between black and white neighborhoods, cities with frozen boundaries had the highest scores. Detroit, for example, had a score of 85, indicating almost complete separation between the races. Syracuse, with a score of 69, was also highly segregated. By contrast, cities whose boundaries had expanded to incorporate suburbs showed a considerable degree of residential integration. Raleigh, for example, scored 46, while Albuquerque came in at an impressive 32. The average degree of separation between rich and poor was also significantly lower in cities that had annexed or consolidated.

These were a minority of cities, however. Nationally, concentrations of poverty increased in the last quarter of the twentieth century. One study of 318 metropolitan areas showed that the number of high-poverty neighborhoods—those with more than 40 percent of residents living below the poverty line—nearly doubled between 1970 and 1990, as poverty spread throughout the cities.[22] There were nearly as many poor whites (14.4 million) as poor blacks and Hispanics (15.7 million) in 2000. Some were rural poor, but almost 80 percent of impoverished Americans, white and minority, lived in metropolitan areas. The contrast between white and nonwhite patterns of residence was stark, however. Whites were more widely dispersed, with three out of four poor whites living in middle-class areas spread across the metropolitan region. But in the case of minorities, 75 percent of poor blacks and 50 percent of poor Hispanics were concentrated in high-poverty inner-city neighborhoods.[23]

David Rusk's 2003 study of metropolitan consolidation found that only fourteen states—six in the West, five in the South, and three in the Midwest—had strong laws authorizing consolidation. He estimated that it would be difficult but possible to achieve some consolidation in eighteen other states.[24] However, consolidation is not the only way to move forward to create more equitable distributions of wealth and to reduce racial isolation. Progress on deconcentrating poverty and increasing racial integration across the urban/suburban boundary has been accomplished in two other important ways in recent decades: fair housing and regional planning.

One of the most impressive steps was taken in Maryland's Montgomery County in 1973, when it adopted a progressive law to ensure that all new housing developments would set aside at least 12 percent of units for rental by poor and lower-income families. The Moderately Priced Dwelling Unit ordinance applied to any subdivision, townhouse development, or apartment complex with more than 35 units. Montgomery County further specified that another 5 percent of the units must be available for rent or purchase by the county housing authority and reserved for families below the poverty line. Private developers set aside more than 11,000 units under the new law.

Thus, Montgomery County had no need to build housing projects—it simply bought standard housing all across the county to rent to poor families. The policy produced no social problems, and the resale value of other homes was unaffected by the inclusion of rental units for the poor within the same development. Moreover, a remarkable social transformation took place. A suburb that was 92 percent white and wealthy in 1970 became one of the nation's most diverse communities by 2000: 16 percent black, 12 percent Hispanic, and 12 percent Asian. It had also become more economically integrated while remaining the thirteenth wealthiest county in America.[25]

Montgomery County acted under a 1927 Maryland law that gave counties strong planning and zoning powers. Three other states—Massachusetts, Connecticut, and New Jersey—later adopted variants of what became known as Fair Share Housing legislation. Both Massachusetts in 1969 and Connecticut in 1989 passed laws to create more affordable housing in the suburbs by providing incentives for builders. In Massachusetts, developers who failed to gain local approval for affordable housing could appeal to the state for an override. Of well over 600,000 new units permitted between 1969 and 2000, over 18,000 of them qualified as affordable—a small but not insignificant number.[26]

Part of the problem with the Massachusetts and Connecticut programs was that they relied on builder initiatives. In a 1983 landmark decision by the New Jersey State Supreme Court, a "fair share" of new housing for the poor was mandated. The Court ruled that zoning prohibitions against affordable housing in the suburban township of Mount Laurel amounted to unconstitutional "economic discrimination," and it set affordable housing targets that developers across the state were required to meet. More than 29,000 affordable units had been set aside in new housing developments by 2002. While that represented a major breakthrough for affordable housing in the suburbs, it was less than 5 percent of all new units built in those decades. If the New Jersey law had adopted the Montgomery County guidelines, it would have increased the fair share of new dwellings for the poor to 46,000. Unlike Montgomery County, Mount Laurel's new affordable housing did not significantly change the level of school segregation. In 2000 New Jersey's elementary schools were ranked as the fifth most racially segregated in the nation.[27]

Portland is justifiably cited as one of the great urban success stories. Its rise was largely due not to housing policy but to a smart transportation and land use policy. Some have flippantly observed that Portland did not want to become another Los Angeles. They are not far off the mark. Oregon's Land Use Act of 1973 stopped the kind of urban sprawl that engulfed Los Angeles and many other cities. Syracuse, for example, kept extending its water and sewer lines and, without land use restrictions, the developers kept coming, too. Oregon required every county to develop land use plans that set boundaries on urban growth and clearly divided urban land from rural land preserved for farming, forestry, and recreation in the wilderness.

The plan developed for the Portland metropolitan region in 1979 established an urban boundary that enclosed 348 square miles. In addition to providing land for current residents in the city and its 23 suburbs, it also allowed space for anticipated residential, commercial, and industrial growth. In 2000, more than 1.3 million people lived within the urban boundary. Less than 5 percent lived in 2,662 square miles of surrounding rural land, where no urbanization was allowed. The Portland plan was highly effective. In the 1990s the city population grew by 18 percent while virtually none of the surrounding farmland was lost.

More important, Portland became a highly desirable place to live and visit. Limits on sprawl caused land values to rise within the boundary and investments in the reuse of older properties to increase. Historic preservation enhanced the urban landscape. Portland became one of the nation's most ethnically and economically integrated cities—a magnet for the "creative class" and high-tech business. Suburban property values were also increased by limiting the availability of cheap land for further development. While Portland grew more dense through attractive mixed-use housing that combined commercial and residential development, it also had cleaner air through improved mass transit and the natural "air conditioning" provided by a wide greenbelt of surrounding forest and farmland.[28]

While fair share housing and regional land use policies had some effect on deconcentrating poverty in the last quarter of the twentieth century, their effect was limited. Many people had hoped that the United States Supreme Court's 1954 decision in *Brown v. Board of Education* outlawing separate schools for blacks and whites in the South would lead to major metropolitan desegregation of schools, and eventually to more racially integrated housing patterns in the suburbs as well.[29] Emboldened by the Supreme Court's decision, New York's Governor Rockefeller in 1960 urged the state legislature to create "federated" or metropolitan school districts. The Syracuse school superintendent embraced Rockefeller's proposal as a "forward step in principle" that would broaden the tax base and reduce the inequalities between city and suburban schools. But the proposal was shelved by the legislature.[30]

In 1971 the Supreme Court ordered desegregation of schools in metropolitan Charlotte, North Carolina, by merging city schools with those of surrounding Mecklenburg County. But just three years later, a more conservative Supreme Court shaped by President Nixon blocked the same remedy for northern cities. With this tragic decision striking down a merger of city and suburban schools in Detroit, the Court effectively blockaded the poor from access to educational equality.[31]

2 Can This Neighborhood Be Saved?

In the late 1970s when my family moved from the suburbs to the city, most residents were heading the other way. Census data later revealed that the exodus from Syracuse reached its peak in that decade. Some of our Skaneateles neighbors, alarmed by newspaper reports of rising crime and failing schools, thought we were putting our children and ourselves at risk by leaving the safety of the suburbs.

But I remembered a thriving city where fathers on my block went off to work at local factories and where a ten-year-old could safely ride his bike for miles through neighborhood streets to play in a grand system of city parks. In the long Syracuse winters we skated on rinks at Kirk Park or Drumlins and sledded in Oakwood, a Frederick Olmsted–inspired cemetery where steep, winding roads ran downhill among huge monuments commemorating the city's prominent citizens. In summer we biked to Onondaga Park on the west side, where a half dozen ponds fed into a small lake, and climbed the ladder of a shiny slide attached to the bathhouse roof, for a thrilling splash into the cool water. Sometimes we played tennis, archery, and ping-pong on the grounds. One summer, my best friend and I built a raft and pushed it with poles down the muddy Onondaga Creek from the edge of the city through Kirk Park to downtown, where we waved triumphantly to onlookers. At MacArthur Field, the city's ballpark where the Syracuse Chiefs played in the International League against Rochester, Montreal, and other cities, families speaking Polish, German, and Italian waited in line at the concession stand for beer and kielbasa or a smoked bratwurst with plenty of mustard and sauerkraut. The only sour note was the booing by some Chiefs fans when Jackie Robinson, then playing for Montreal, first walked on the field.

Whatever concerns I had in the 1970s were tempered by my experience of growing up in the city and attending Central High School in the 1950s with many poor and working-class black students. I did not fear African Americans in the way that some of our suburban neighbors did. Not that the city of my youth was free from racism. My own family never used the "N" word, and I felt we were free of such prejudice until I brought a black classmate home one day to help me write a speech. John Patterson had been student president of the school, and he was a great speaker. I hoped to succeed him (though as it turned out I was whomped in the election). After John left our house, I was shocked when my father said to me, "It's all right to go to school with them, but don't bring them home. You don't want one of them to marry your sister, do you?"

I also knew something about gangs and crime. My brother, Jimmy, was in the numbers racket, spent time in jail, and died of a heroin overdose at age 39. My uncle, Joseph Grant, had been a leader of a gang on the city's west side and spent most of his life in Auburn State Prison for killing a police officer in a shoot-out during a warehouse burglary. It was a banner headline in the Syracuse newspapers. My father, a former steelworker and then a salesman at Wells and Coverly, a leading men's clothing store, did not want to go to work that day, but my mother insisted he show up and do his job. He was glad he did. Apparently the publicity helped—he worked on commission, and sales that day turned out to be quite high.

I thought of myself as a street-wise academic professional, who saw suburban fears as exaggerated and who appreciated the benefits of city life: a first-class symphony, a major university, a lively arts community, and a park system that was less well maintained than in the 1950s but still impressive. I didn't realize it at the time, but as we looked at houses in Syracuse something deep inside me began to stir. I had lived a cosmopolitan life in New York City, Washington, D.C., and Brookline, Massachusetts, and when we came back to upstate New York, I had bought a large house safely cordoned off in an upscale village eighteen miles from the grime and crime of Syracuse. In many ways I had deliberately severed myself from my origins. I couldn't say that with the move to Westcott I was finally returning home, because much of that world was gone. But I was reconnecting with some deep roots, reclaiming a part of myself that had been buried.

In my twenties, brimming with energy and idealism, I had once thought about coming back to Syracuse to run for mayor. I went to see my uncle, James Hanley, the first Democratic congressman elected from Syracuse in fifty-two years. Over lunch in the House dining room, he laid out the steps I would need to take.[1] That dream languished as three children came along and I felt confirmed in my life as a writer and teacher. Yet the part of me that wanted to break out of a world of observation and analysis and into the world of engagement and action had never been completely extinguished. I no longer had any desire to be a mayor, but perhaps I could help save a neighborhood.

I did not have the wisdom to see the future that would unfold, nor did I realize how much the city had already crumbled. I came to understand that the changes in Syracuse were more pervasive and destructive of a good community than I could ever have imagined. Although I knew that the 1960s had changed the American cultural landscape, I did not grasp the multiple and overlapping social pathologies that were scarring major cities until my own children became enmeshed in them.

The increasing concentration and isolation of the urban poor was perhaps the most devastating development, along with the abandonment of inner-city housing to the ravages of rot, drug addicts, and homeless squatters. The 1960s story of sex, drugs, and disrespect for authority among middle-class baby boomers has become gospel, especially among conservative writers. It is less often noted that the rebelliousness of this period affected teenagers and children in suburban and rural areas as well as those in cities. Divorce and illegitimacy rates rose among whites as well as blacks. Drug use increased in some suburban schools as much or more than it did in city high schools. But in urban environments like Syracuse, opportunity shrank and pathology deepened for children in ways that suburban children would never know. The concentration of poverty and unemployment led to a loss of authority in schools and more incivility on the streets. Networks of support were much more deeply frayed in city neighborhoods, and in some they virtually collapsed. Suburban children were buffered from the strife of racial integration that ravaged the public schools of Boston, Syracuse, and many other urban systems.

My family's move to Westcott was not intended to become a social experiment. We did not pick the neighborhood as a scientific sample of the civic challenges of that era. I never planned to write about our lives as "urban pioneers." But as it turned out, Westcott was a microcosm of city life in the last quarter of the twentieth century—neither slum nor suburb, it was a diverse neighborhood bordered by a major housing project in one direction and Syracuse University in the other. The story of Westcott is a tale of neighborhood change on the streets and in the schools, of decline and distress, followed by community development and the struggles of renewal. While community action was able to slow Westcott's disintegration and attract some reinvestment, the long arc of deepening poverty in the city and its schools still looms over the neighborhood where my wife and I still live.

Except for a minor upset when our son's bicycle was stolen, our first months in the city were a honeymoon. I was on a ladder a lot in the summer of 1978, painting the house before we moved in, and I enjoyed hearing stories about the history of the neighborhood from passers-by. My wife loved her new job at King Elementary about a mile away, and I enjoyed the walk to my office at the university. Westcott had the virtues of a small urban village where our children could bike to the park. Trolley tracks could still be seen beneath tarred-over Westcott Street— our main street. It was lined with a supermarket, drugstore, five and dime, florist shop, tailor, watch and shoe repair, dry cleaner, movie theater, postal substation, used-book store, Chinese takeout, and two restaurants. Our eldest daughter, by then 18, waitressed at Bojangles, where many of our friends gathered for breakfast on Sunday mornings to kibitz and read *The New York Times*. The Petit Branch Library and Westcott Community Center were popular meeting places as well. Within a few blocks from Westcott were a neighborhood elementary school and a junior high. There were two large churches, one Baptist and the other Methodist, as well as a Quaker Meeting House. The sizable Jewish community was anchored by a synagogue and a Jewish Community Center with a gymnasium and swimming pool.

Signs of some neighborhood decay could be detected, especially as one neared the Rolling Green Estates housing project to the north—houses needing paint, cluttered porches, sagging steps, littered lawns. Over the next decade the exodus that had already decimated other areas of the city began to hit Westcott as well. The visual trash of "For Sale" and "For Rent" signs spread. Desperate landlords did less careful screening of tenants. When gangs and drug-running made Rolling Green Estates unsafe, frightened welfare families used their Section 8 vouchers to move into vacated houses in the neighborhood. Many buildings became overcrowded with poor families, refugees, and university students. Sofas and piles of trash started to accumulate on front porches that had once been tidy and welcoming. Grass grew knee-high around some houses. Tenants started to park on lawns and block sidewalks with their automobiles. They pushed shopping carts up the streets and then abandoned them in vacant lots.

As tension began to flare on some blocks, screaming and vulgar language grew louder. Boyfriends banged on doors. Some drug-runners shouted threats as they tried to collect on debts. Cops often pulled "suspects" out of houses. It reminded me of times when the police came to our house on Warner Avenue looking for my brother Jimmy, sometimes getting him out of bed to take him downtown for questioning. Their flashing lights in our driveway mortified my mother, who pled with the cops as they dragged "Red" out the door. But we were the only family on our block where this kind of thing happened. In Westcott, it happened frequently.

Panhandlers rang doorbells at all hours. Many of us gave freely as mothers told stories about needing money for diapers or medicine—until we began to learn that four or five neighbors had bought diapers for the same woman on the same night. We got tougher and tried to draw a line between panhandlers and people with real needs. And there were many of the latter. We commiserated about how uneasy it made us to live so close to people who were so poor. Talk about diversity is easy, from a distance, but it's painful to see the faces of poverty at your front door.

As the years passed, both poverty and violence rose unabated. There were no full-scale riots within the Westcott neighborhood, but tensions on the streets escalated. Black teenagers from the project congregated angrily in front of a neighborhood market that employed no African Americans, and by morning some of the windows were broken. Less violent but more frightening were young toughs who would take the last swig from a bottle and, raising their arms in a great arc, jump in the air to smash the bottle on the sidewalk or the street, daring those sitting on porches nearby to say anything about it. Fewer and fewer did. In a display of boom-box terror, cars with powerful speakers cruised through the neighborhood at all hours with speakers turned to the max, loud enough to rattle your windows. Some neighbors who left said this particular kind of torture was the last straw for them.

Gangs from the project began to swing heavy chains, and one night the windows in a long block of parked cars were smashed with tire irons. Yet inexplicably we did not really grasp what was happening to our family life until we returned to the neighborhood after a summer vacation. We settled in for the evening with a good movie, and later, as I walked a few blocks to return the video, I saw three boys in their midteens coming up the street. They were jumping up to break off overhanging branches, and one of them had a thick stick about a yard long that he was using to whack everything in sight. As they got to the small string of stores near the commercial district, the boy with the stick began swinging at a hanging sign for the auto repair shop. A few pieces of plastic fell to the sidewalk. A man about forty years old came out of a house and crossed the street just ahead of me. When he got close to the teenagers, they paused and looked at him intently. But they broke into smiles when he yelled, "Go for it, man!" His voice was slurred from drugs or alcohol. They happily resumed whacking away. The next morning, I saw that half the sign was in shreds.

This incident was part of an escalating pattern of incivility that included urinating on lawns, attacking gays, and threatening anyone who complained about such behavior. Once when our daughter was walking home from school, a young thug ripped a gold chain from her neck. Other gang members beat up our son—twice. Yet as other whites fled the neighborhood, we stayed.

By the end of the 1980s the percentage of owner-occupied housing in Westcott had dropped by half, reflecting wholesale middle-class flight, and much of the business district had gone dark. The drug store, dry cleaner, shoe repair, supermarket, variety store, Bojangles, and other retail establishments were gone. The theater that had once shown art films had become a porno movie house. The funeral home had reopened as a bar. A liquor store stood on the lot of what had once been a gas station. But by this time my wife and I had brought together a group of neighbors to form an organization to renew the neighborhood. We began to think about why neighborhoods collapse and what could be done to save ours.

Social Capital

My own earlier work had been a study of the theories of James Coleman, a sociologist who had written about the importance of the human relationships and supportive networks that enrich the cognitive and social development of children and sustain the norms of a good community. Take away those relationships—the "glue" that holds civil society together—and we progressively reduce our ability to take effective cooperative action toward any goal.

Coleman called these networks and relationships "social capital." It is not the same as human capital or physical capital. Physical capital refers to land that produces crops or to machines that facilitate the production of goods. Human capital comprises the skills and knowledge that individuals have learned so that they can do things others will pay for. Social capital is less tangible: it is created among people who trust one another and set standards of behavior for the group. If people come together to do things in a way that develops trust among them—by forming a bowling league, for example—they create more social capital for themselves, which they can "spend" or invest in communal efforts such as opening a food coop or prohibiting parties of teenagers when no adult is home.

Even more than the closing of stores and other gathering places, Westcott's social capital was depleted by the closing of the neighborhood elementary school as part of a citywide racial integration plan. There was no longer a public school in Westcott to bring parents together across race and class lines. Parents of young children have the highest attendance at school events and volunteer more often in the classroom and in other school projects. By engaging in face-to-face interaction around grade-school issues, parents are more likely to develop the trust that is essential for establishing shared norms and common expectations in the larger community.

Another blow to Westcott's social capital came when the synagogue and Jewish recreation center moved to the suburbs. This withdrew not only services for youth but also the presence on the street of a strongly integrated community that helped model good behavior throughout the neighborhood. At a time when Westcott's need for supportive networks of concerned parents and citizens had never been higher, social capital and other resources were in sharp decline. The ratio of adult caregivers to poor children had shifted dramatically, and not for the better. This put at even greater risk a significant number of children who were already victims of inadequate prenatal care, drug or alcohol abuse, and family stress from frequent moves. In 1950, 10 percent of the population in the Rolling Green census tract was fourteen years old or younger, but by 1980 that percentage had doubled to 23, while the number of adults ages 25 to 44 had fallen by half. Group homes for teenagers proliferated as some parents gave up trying to control their children, declaring them "persons in need of supervision" by the state.

My research assistant, Jennifer Esposito, helped me see a more fine-grained analysis of life in the Westcott neighborhood as experienced by the children who lived there. This portrait emerged from twenty-three interviews with Westcott youth, most of them teenagers. Ten of the interviewees were white and nine were black. The remaining four declared themselves to be Puerto Rican, Native American, East Indian, and "Blackinese"—part African American and part Japanese.[2] The aim of the research was to assess the social capital of these teenagers and to discover how they negotiated their world. Each teenager was conceptualized as being at the hub of a wheel, and each relationship or bond the teen had with another person was a spoke in that wheel. We were particularly interested in what supportive relationships teenagers had with adults—parents or guardians, mentors in youth organizations, coaches, music teachers, ministers, or people at work who took an interest in them. We found that different teenagers within the same neighborhood had radically different "wheels."

Some had parents who were only occasionally present in their lives and had virtually no other positive bonds with adults. Yet even some of these teenagers saw Westcott as a supportive neighborhood. A few of them had moved there from more crime-ridden and poverty-stricken parts of the city. One teen, Beppy, was aware of Westcott's liberal reputation and told us that people there were friendlier and more laid-back: "Nobody gets bent out of shape here. You feel safe here . . . You can go outside at 5 in the morning and be safe from gunshots . . . You walk around here and people have gardens and things." These youths were living mostly on their own. They smoked dope, did a little hustling, got "toasted" in a nearby park where they spent a lot of time. "We're like brothers. We normally kick it, go out, go to parties, get drunk. We always watch each other. If we all end up going to a park and somebody gets drunk, you know, we always watch after them. We never let him leave our side if he wants to go and pick a fight. But we don't pick a fight. The fights always come to us."

They carried weapons on occasion. But more often, like Beppy and his friends, they traveled with a Doberman or other attack dog trained to do serious damage on command. Guns were supposedly for protection only. Beppy explained: "If they pull a gun on me, all right, I am not the kind of person that would get scared . . . But if they put the gun away I am going back to my house and get my gun and just not show it to them." There had been shootings, and two teens were killed in a fight near a corner known for drug dealing.

The good life was getting high and hanging out, mixed with some "excitement" when things got draggy—spraying graffiti on a wall or stealing mail to get a credit card or hitting on some girl. But Beppy insisted he didn't steal for the thrills. "Cause I don't get no thrill out of it. You know, unless I am getting paid, then I'll take it; if not, then I won't take it." Beppy said he had no goals in life other than to get a lot of money. When pressed, he mocked us by saying that his goal was to "die and come back a leopard." Then, more seriously, he added that he liked music and wanted to be "a singer, a rapper," a big recording star. He looked to no one for advice:

> Interviewer: Is your mom the most influential person in your life?
> Beppy: Most what?
> Interviewer: Influential, a person that you rely on most for advice?
> Beppy: No.
> Interviewer: Who is?
> Beppy: Me.
> Interviewer: You? So you are on your own.
> Beppy: Yep.

Several teenagers we interviewed had jobs in fast-food joints and cited someone at work they could turn to for help, maybe. But other than an occasional employer, no one was holding these kids accountable, expecting them to work hard or measure up to any ideals. Neither teachers nor cops were trusted; on the contrary, they were regarded as part of the opposition. To be seen as cooperating or being compliant with authority figures diminished a person's respect on the street. Although they were likely to have siblings or cousins who had been imprisoned, most of these teenagers had not yet been locked up. Still, they were into the life of the street or headed that way.

Within the same neighborhood were a diminishing number of teenagers, both black and white, who had many positive bonds

47

with adults: parents who set curfews and supervised homework, coaches who were demanding, teachers whom they trusted and respected, along with advisers at church and at work. TJ was an African-American teenager who had recently graduated from high school when we interviewed him. Though his parents were not Catholic, they had sent him to parochial school after he began to hang out with some boys who were veering toward street life. TJ's parents feared that things would go badly for him if he remained in a public school. He did well in his new school, after an initial struggle. The academic demands were a wake-up call: he had been getting straight As but now got Cs. "It was a lot more work so I had to make higher expectations for myself." He started getting a few Bs his sophomore year and ended his senior year with mostly As and Bs and a college scholarship.

TJ occasionally saw his old middle-school friends, who were still in the neighborhood, but it wasn't the same as before. "Well, a lot of them are, you know, on the streets now. Selling drugs, maybe not selling drugs, but smoking weed or whatever and they are not really into school. They are not headed in the same direction as me and it's kinda sad; you look and you see the people I grew up with. We all had the same goals when we started. We kinda drifted away . . . Oh, I do see them walking around and stuff. I will ask them what they are doing next year and they are like, 'I didn't even graduate, you know, I am just trying to get a job and stuff.'" At the time we interviewed him, TJ believed that many of his old friends would have liked to go to college, and he felt sad that they were being left behind. He was quick to reassure us that they had as much academic ability as he did. "I just feel bad 'cause it seems like something they want to do. I mean its not like they are stupid or anything . . . We were all together and we all did well in school. I guess they just got involved in the wrong things."

We asked why he had not suffered his friends' fate. TJ didn't hesitate: "My parents, they really wanted me to get an education. Education was always first. Always do your homework. They was always, I was just, I just always did it. It was just like second nature. I didn't want to fail at anything. I didn't want to let my parents down. It was like, you know, I had temptations, but I just knew it was something my parents wouldn't want me to get into." There was no sliding by: "My mom has always been on me to work every night. She comes home and asks if I have my work done. I'm like 'Yeah,' and she says, 'Let me see it.' She will check over it. She taught me how to type, and my dad got me a computer."

Perhaps half the children in the neighborhood fell somewhere between Beppy and TJ. They had not yet adopted Beppy's street life, but they did not have the rich networks of support that kept TJ out of trouble and in school. Many of them lived in Rolling Green Estates or in subsidized apartments or houses in deteriorating areas of the neighborhood. There might have been one parent at home who was working two jobs to make ends meet. Younger siblings were unsupervised after dark and sometimes rode their tricycles into the street. They missed medical checkups, and their health suffered. Those in school came home to empty apartments. Sometimes their mother would find time to make supper between jobs, but much of the time children ate from fast-food containers, sitting in front of the television.

Steve Susman, director of the Westcott Community Center for nearly a decade and a person who knew the youth of the neighborhood as well as anybody, felt that "wholesale change, radical change" was needed to reach more of the children in poverty. "We need to grab the kids before they get tied up in gangs and drugs." He wanted to develop more programs to get teenagers on career tracks, and provide more internships to show them the variety of careers open to them and what it would take to qualify for such jobs. Current programs, he said, were reaching only a small fraction of the children in the neighborhood who needed them.[3]

Without more spokes in their wheels, few youths like Beppy were going to make it. They would continue to watch TV or pass a joint instead of tackling math homework. Skipping school was easy. Girls with low social capital were more likely to get pregnant, especially in a culture where the old sanctions against sexual activity no longer applied. Boys who wanted to achieve would be tested by what Elijah Anderson called the "code of the street."[4] Although they may not have intended to cross the line into the kind of petty crime that Beppy's brothers considered standard stuff, they would often adopt the swagger and low-hanging pants and trademark boots or jogging shoes that the brothers displayed. This sent a signal: "Don't mess with me. I deserve respect." The lure of the street was powerful, and the brothers were cool. To prove you were cool too, you might have to break some windows and maybe deliver some drugs. Later, you might not be able to resist an offer of crack cocaine. "Try this, you can handle it."

You learned to disguise achievement in school and to "code switch"—to shift linguistic gears and body language as you moved from talking with teachers to passing by Beppy's crowd on the street corner. You switched without thinking from an attitude of deference to a posture of defiance. And having no other supports or voices to stop your slide, you began skipping school and falling behind in math. You had hoped to go to college, and maybe you still would. But this way of becoming a man by becoming a brother—getting some cash and a car and the "props" that go with it—might be okay for a while. You could go to college later. Sure.

Hamilton High

When major desegregation of public schools began in the late 1960s, adolescents from Rolling Green Estates began to enter previously all-white Hamilton High—a school where I did research over a twenty-year period, including teaching there for two years in the mid-1980s and again, more briefly, in 2003–2005.[5] Proponents assumed that racial integration would end isolation for both black and white students. They thought desegregation would be particularly beneficial to African Americans, who would have access to an enriched curriculum taught by what was widely regarded as an elite teaching faculty.

Those hopes were realized for some students, especially middle-class blacks who lived outside the housing projects. But disproportionate numbers of students from Rolling Green Estates were placed in a dead-end track of diluted classwork and low expectations. They left predominantly black schools where they had felt successful socially, only to enter a virtually closed social system of white fraternities and sororities. They had to make their way in an environment where they were labeled as losers in the classroom and were politely shunned in the hallways. They came together with whites only to learn how far behind they had been in their de facto segregated elementary and junior high schools.

The black presence at Hamilton High escalated rapidly under a desegregation plan limited to city schools, eventually accounting for nearly half of enrollment, while suburban schools remained virtually all white. In the fall of 1968, after a memorial service for Martin Luther King Jr., a riot broke out at Hamilton. African-American students rampaged through the school, destroying equipment in a physics laboratory and tearing into the library, where they overturned tables, swept books off the shelves, smashed windows, and tore up floor tiles. School was closed ten times that year because of various clashes. The yawning gap between desegregation and integration was evident for all to see. Paid aides and a policeman were permanently stationed in the school, and during the few minutes of informal contact when black and white students passed in the halls between classes, faculty members held their breath. Hamilton, like other recently desegregated high schools in the city, went on block sessions: classes were shortened and school ended at 1:00 p.m. so that students could be sent home for lunch rather than risk confrontations in the cafeteria. Assemblies were canceled for more than a decade. There were no school dances at Hamilton High.

Consultants were brought in to open discussions between black and white students. Many children of liberal white parents who favored integration in principle vented their anger about the lewd remarks blacks made in hallways and expressed fear that blacks were "ruining our school." African Americans detailed incidents of racism by teachers who "had given up" on them and by fellow students who had rebuffed them. The principal at that time summed up the discussions: "There was an awful lot of hate involved there . . . and there was some progress. It was brought about by whites and blacks alike being forced to say just who the hell are you and what are you doing? And who the hell are you with all your money? And who the hell are you trying to break up my school?"[6]

Many teachers felt they were failures, ill-equipped to teach the large number of poorly prepared black students who now sat in their classrooms. The strategies they had previously employed no longer worked. They lacked the knowledge, resourcefulness, imagination, and energy to reach these often angry black teenagers. Some teachers, especially middle-aged white men, admitted their fear and confessed their inability to establish order in their classrooms. They were ground down, exhausted, defeated, and confused. By fall 1971, almost three quarters of the teachers who had taught at Hamilton High in 1966 had resigned, retired, or transferred.

If social capital lies in stable human relationships, this huge turnover of teachers and principals represented a huge loss. It weakened ties between parents and the school, and once those relationships were frayed, mutual expectations about academic achievement and homework as well as standards of behavior went by the wayside. Younger replacement teachers, some of whom smoked marijuana with students at parties, were at odds with the more traditional teachers who stayed on. The faculty, which had formerly eaten lunch together in the teachers' lounge, now split into three factions. Teachers were unsure whether their new colleagues would back them up if they challenged a disruptive student in the halls.

In the span of a decade, nearly half of middle-class students left Hamilton High for the suburbs. Some parents of those who remained chained the doors of the school one morning to express their frustration that the school was no longer a fit or safe place for their children to enter. Black and white parents did not meet, as they once had, to help plan social events at the school, for these had been canceled for years. Without dances to chaperone, clubs to advise, and athletic events to attend, parents had little opportunity to come together and develop the trust and sense of common aims that are essential for the growth of social capital. Without school-sponsored extracurricular activities, students—black and white—were severely deprived of opportunities to extend their social networks and to exercise leadership abilities in ways they had at their former schools. Only recently have African-American analysts like Vanessa Siddle Walker focused on these kinds of losses when black schools were closed.[7]

Within the Westcott neighborhood, tensions rose and violence increased on the streets. More windows were broken and police were called. More bottles were smashed on sidewalks by youths who sauntered by with boom boxes blaring from shoulder straps. Boys only nine or ten years old did "wheelies" on their bicycles, pirouetting in front of cars that had come to a corner stop sign, keeping drivers at bay for several minutes. Scared whites, like many teachers at Hamilton High, often did nothing except lock their car doors.

By the end of the 1970s the evaporation of social capital from Westcott was severe. Among those whites migrating to the segregated suburbs were teachers at Hamilton High, who had seen the problems first-hand and wanted a more predictable learning environment for their children. The exodus of whites slowed in the 1980s, and Hamilton High finally stabilized, as did other city schools in the second decade after desegregation plans were put into effect. Our son had left for a year to attend a Catholic school, but he missed his old friends. He returned to Hamilton during the middle of his sophomore year and became president of his class. By then, relations between black and white students had improved markedly. The days when parents had to put chains on the doors were a distant memory shared by only a few, and unknown to most students who now attended the school. These students, black and white, had gone to elementary and middle school together—an advantage that the first students to desegregate Syracuse schools had not enjoyed. Conditions in the school were more conducive to learning, and African-American students were better prepared to take advanced classes in math and science. Yet large gaps in achievement levels and dropout rates between whites and minorities remained.

Most schools remained racially balanced through the 1980s. Although the percentage of black residents in the northern half of Westcott increased to 55 percent by 1990, all but 5 percent of that increase had occurred by 1980. But poverty had steadily worsened, with 17 percent of the population in poverty in 1970, 22 percent in 1980, and 47 percent in 1990. Yet there was a glimmer of hope: in the southern tract nearest the university, some middle-class whites with children had returned to the neighborhood, and considerable gentrification and restoration of historic homes had been undertaken, much of it by gay and lesbian couples.

Rebuilding Community

One measure of social capital in a neighborhood is the number of gathering places where residents meet to talk and interact—shops, coffeehouses, libraries, bars, bookstores. In my old Brighton neighborhood, the loss of social capital, measured this way, was devastating. In 1950 there had been 101 shops and gathering places in the six-block heart of the Brighton business district. By 1989 only 38 were left.[8] The loss was far less severe but nonetheless real in the Westcott neighborhood. Part of Westcott's appeal was the urban-village feel of coffeehouses, bookshops, and a movie theater. One expected to meet friends on the way to the newsstand or in the café after a movie. Most of this was gone by the early 1980s. Almost half of Westcott's two-block business district was vacant. Two new taverns and three pizza shops had opened up, but the area was now dreary and poorly lighted at night.

The conversion of a good neighborhood theater into a porn house might have been the final straw that led to the founding of the Westcott East Neighborhood Association. Members made plain from the beginning that this would not be just another neighborhood watch group, as important as those might be, but would engage in community development on a broad scale. Robert Haley, a distinguished local architect, took a leading role in developing a plan for a pedestrian-friendly neighborhood. In his vision, wider sidewalks in the business district would slow down traffic; greenways would link the library with other areas of the neighborhood; flower boxes, benches, tree plantings, and even more attractive trash bins would do their part to draw people out of their homes and into common spaces. Dozens of neighbors came together to trim overgrown trees and bushes and clear trash from empty lots so that gardens could be designed and planted. They raised money for landscaping around the library by selling bricks for the garden plaza engraved with donors' names.

As membership in the neighborhood association grew, task forces were formed. One developed a simple checklist drawn from city codes that was used to inspect every home in the neighborhood for broken windows, cluttered sidewalks, missing porch steps, piled up trash, and other violations. Many citations were issued, and before long the neighborhood started to see a fresh coat of paint on shabby dwellings and fewer boarded-up windows. Even people who were not cited began to make improvements after seeing that their neighbors were willing to reinvest in their property.

We rated streets, curbs, and sidewalks and took photographs with us to the mayor's office. We asked his aides how people could be convinced to buy homes in Westcott when their cars fell into potholes as they drove into the neighborhood. Within a few years streets were repaved, sidewalks were repaired, and curbs were replaced. A model lease was developed to prevent absentee landlords from posting garish for-rent signs and from allowing tenants to park cars on lawns. The neighborhood association also tried to emphasize the positive, by giving awards for the most improved house or storefront, the most beautiful garden, and the most notable community service. We made these award ceremonies the occasion for coming together at neighborhood parties and encouraging others to join our efforts. We invited city officials to our celebrations as well as to our committee meetings. The police chief, city council members, county officials, code enforcement officers, and others came to Westcott frequently, to speak and answer questions.

State, city, and some federal funds were tapped to help revive the neighborhood. Two nonprofit organizations, Housing Visions and East Side Neighbors in Partnership, made significant improvements by rehabilitating housing on several blocks. A neighborhood preservation association obtained funds from the university and the city to offer low-cost guaranteed mortgages to low-income live-in owners. In its first ten years, this program led to the conversion of more than three hundred rental dwellings, many of them poorly maintained, to owner-occupied housing.

Meanwhile, the Westcott Community Development Corporation helped to revivify the business district. Over the course of a decade the movie theater was renovated and reopened under new ownership, drawing good crowds for first-run films. Several new eateries opened, serving Middle Eastern, Mexican, and Chinese food. A new art gallery and framing shop took over the old hardware store site; a specialty clothing store moved into the storefront once occupied by the five-and-dime. Efforts to attract a new supermarket to the neighborhood were unsuccessful, but a small convenience store opened as part of a pizza-and-beer outlet. The old supermarket, vacant for nearly three years, was attractively transformed into a daycare center for disabled adults. The Westcott Community Center renovated a two-story brick building that had been a city fire station and began to offer programs for teenagers and the elderly there. The Westcott East Neighborhood Association drew teenagers into art and garden projects.

The rebirth of the community became apparent to the wider metropolitan area as a result of two public relations efforts. The first was a two-page spread in Syracuse newspapers heralding the first Westcott house tour of renovated and restored historic homes. The event sold out, drawing hundreds of visitors to the neighborhood, many of whom would have hesitated to walk around the area two decades earlier. The second effort was the Westcott Cultural Fair, celebrating the neighborhood's diversity. It began on a small scale, then became an annual event that featured dozens of musical performances, arts and crafts, ethnic foods, and information on community activities. It opened with a parade during which the mayor and city council members marched with children from the Westcott community, along with mummers, dancers, and bands. Members of the neighborhood association, holding a banner encouraging new members to enroll, walked along shouting, "We are the New Urban Village! Help us grow." The daylong event drew more than 3,000 residents and visitors. At a curbside table, the neighborhood association signed up new members and sold postcards showing the variety of murals, gardens, and other successful projects undertaken. One of the best-sellers was a photograph of more than a dozen fireplugs painted in brilliant stripes and patterns by a neighborhood artist.

The loss of social capital was partially reversed in Westcott, and renewal of the neighborhood was real. That was no small achievement. But the academic gains Hamilton High experienced in the 1980s were also partially explained by the growth of social capital in the neighborhood. A new black principal won strong support from parents when he instituted codes for dress and behavior. Most parents stood behind him when some critics complained that too many students were being suspended for infractions. Teachers did not believe that he would be able to get students to take off their baseball caps indoors, but within a week the hats were gone in a school where they had become an emblem of casual cool in the classroom. After explaining to each class of students why he felt the change was necessary to improve the climate of the school, the principal stood at the front door every morning politely but firmly telling students they must remove their caps or give them up.

Evidence of a new consensus emerged during a dispute on a block where several poor families, most of them black, had recently moved with the aid of Section 8 housing vouchers. They were not the first black residents; the block had been about one fourth African American for some time. But now there was evidence of drug activity in two of the newly rented houses, along with young children playing on the street late into the night unsupervised, and music blaring at all hours. A resident of one house was arrested on crack cocaine charges. Neighbors complained that the landlord, who owned many rental properties in Westcott, would take any tenant, no matter how irresponsible, because the Section 8 vouchers guaranteed a steady stream of rental income. The landlord accused the neighbors of being racists, and his accusations were reported in the Syracuse newspapers. But blacks in the neighborhood spoke out against the landlord, including the editor of an African-American weekly. Section 8 subsidies for the two houses were subsequently denied, triggering a countersuit by the landlord. An investigation by the regional New York–New Jersey HUD office concluded that "both minorities and non-minorities interviewed" did not feel that race was an issue in the neighborhood complaints.[9]

The neighbors on that block were raising basic questions about the care and supervision of children, and the old race card did not play. Both white scholars like Christopher Jencks and Susan Mayer and black intellectuals such as William Julius Wilson and Glenn Loury have addressed these issues in their research.[10] Black ministers and civil rights leaders have become more willing to speak publicly about the need to strengthen family responsibility in the black community and to urge parents to read to their children, turn off the television, and make a space in the kitchen where children can do homework. Although the erosion of such practices may be most severe among the poor, it affects many in the middle class as well, where parents working long hours may be unable to spend as much time with their children as they would like. Students from rich as well as poor families have high levels of drug and alcohol abuse. All families need help, though some more than others. New structures of support are necessary.

As faith-based social reforms gained new ground during the late 1990s, it appeared that the Westcott neighborhood might benefit. An African-American woman who converted to Islam developed a proposal to take over the management of Rolling Green Estates. She had been a branch manager of a bank in New York City, and after moving to Syracuse to work in real estate she became actively engaged in many inner-city reform efforts. She wanted to establish a mission or settlement house within the housing project, run by a tenant council. She planned to offer classes in prenatal and postnatal care, organize childcare support groups, and open a food pantry with cooking classes geared toward a healthy diet, as well as make a place for religious services of all denominations within the project. Unfortunately, she was turned down on the grounds that she had no previous experience in managing a large housing project.

The efforts of community organizations in Westcott to create new jobs, reverse the decline of the commercial district, rehabilitate housing, and initiate a variety of community projects helped to stop the downward slide of children at risk in two important ways. First, they reconstituted and strengthened good norms, by bringing people together, face-to-face, to talk about common problems and to decide what kind of action to take. As organizations grew in Westcott, one could attend a community meeting almost any night of the week. Heated arguments often broke out about poor policing or what to do about a proposed zoning change for a new super-drugstore with a drive-in window that would sell beer as well as pharmaceuticals. Some people left in a huff. But like the lively town meetings still held throughout New England today, these discussions and disagreements represented the best of democracy at work, and eventually led to agreements that improved standards of living for the entire neighborhood.

Policing was a critical issue. By comparing stories, neighbors learned that other residents had stopped calling the Police Department to complain about noise or suspected drug trafficking because officers would show up only after many complaints. Residents had become fed up with a 911 system of high-tech policing that was designed to respond quickly to violent crimes but hardly at all to broken windows. They complained about a triage system that directed routine neighborhood complaints to a tape recorder for later transcribing. "Why are there no foot patrols?" Westcott citizens asked. A community police officer began attending most meetings of the Westcott Neighborhood Association, which by that point had enrolled nearly two hundred dues-paying members. Over a period of several years police became more attentive to what Fred Siegel called the "moral regulation of public space."[11] Foot patrols were started on weekends under a private grant secured by the Westcott Community Development Center.

Surveillance combined with real sanctions were necessary to secure safe streets and decent behavior. By 2000 the change in Westcott was noticeable, although incidents of wilding still occurred. Citizens understood that urban streets had always been contested terrain, as Peter Baldwin reminded us in his study of Hartford reforms in the nineteenth century.[12] They also knew that the community could not rely solely on giving police a bigger stick. Westcott community organizations learned to be proactive. Rather than expecting parents to come to us, we took our meetings to the street. For example, we held a block party on Harvard Place, where high turnover had brought in many new Section 8 tenants. More than sixty residents, about a third of them African American, came to enjoy ice cream sundaes. They were all asked to answer two questions posted on large charts tacked to a porch railing: What do we like about Harvard Place? What would make Harvard Place a *better* place? The questions generated a lively discussion.

Residents appreciated many things about their block. One child who had moved there from Rolling Green Estates liked being on a block with porches where people said hello when he walked by. To make it a better place, a nine-year-old black girl asked that people coming down the street "stop using so many curse words and stop breaking bottles on the sidewalk." Everyone applauded. A vote was taken to define the top three priorities for improving the block: demolishing a burned-out house, planting more flowers, and painting a badly peeling house. Everyone also pledged to support the nine-year-old girl's plea not to sit idly by when they saw bottles being smashed on their street or sidewalks. By the end of the year several neighborhood organizations cooperated to accomplish all three objectives of the poll.[13]

The second-most essential action taken by Westcott's neighborhood organizations was to bring people together across racial and generational lines to work on community improvement projects that were visible to all. It was important to go beyond talk at an ice cream party to action on Harvard Place. More than a dozen black and white residents got on ladders to paint the dilapidated house, and everyone saw flowers planted and new bike racks installed to cut down on thefts. The work reinforced new relationships, as neighbors lent each other tools and steadied ladders.

Projects that cross generational lines, putting children in positive relationships with adults, were also critical to mending the frayed social networks in Westcott. One of the most successful involved hundreds of children and adults in making tiles for a community mural. Public tables were set up so that adults and children, sitting side-by-side, could paint and glaze them. Teenagers became acquainted with adults who later hired them to mow lawns or paint a garage, or recommended them to a potential employer. Many of the adults who participated were retirees who had not previously found such a congenial setting for interacting with children from other parts of the community. Some of the most active board members of neighborhood organizations were in their seventies. When the mural was completed, we held a party to celebrate in a coffeehouse next to the building where the mural was affixed to the wall.

Not all of our efforts succeeded. An ambitious endeavor to create a neighborhood center of the arts and technology by renovating the vacant Jewish War Veterans Home raised the hopes of many. Plans were made to create spaces for painting, filmmaking, sculpture, audio recording, and a community FM radio station. Some artists would live in a wing of the building and serve as mentors to the young. But poor management of initial funding grants eventually killed the project.

In another initiative, the neighborhood association hoped to purchase run-down houses, employ teenagers to help with rehabilitation, and then sell them as affordable homes. Young workers from the projects and more affluent parts of the neighborhood would work together, earn money, and learn new skills as masons, carpenters, painters, drywallers, and plumbers. Thirty residents pledged a thousand dollars each to buy the first house. But the project fell apart over legal issues: the difficulties of incorporation and liability for injuries or accidents. Another plan involved purchasing a sidewalk snowplow and hiring teenagers to plow all the walks in the neighborhood after a storm. Some suburbs had plowed all their sidewalks for years, but in Westcott liability issues once again killed the plan. Elderly residents and the children of Westcott continued to walk in the streets, which were safer than the icy sidewalks that absentee landlords and less civic-minded homeowners failed to shovel.

Why Neighborhood Activists Cannot Do It All

Strengthening a sense of family responsibility and generating new social capital are vital to the preservation of a community, but they are not enough to turn the larger demographic tide. Reclaimed neighborhoods in cities like Syracuse are islands of success in a slowly rising sea of poverty. The middle class in Westcott continued to shrink, as poverty deepened decade by decade in the city as a whole. A trickle of gentrification led to the conversion of some historic buildings into attractive apartments downtown, but vast areas of the city remained desolate. Two upscale high-rise apartments built just a block away from the Everson Art Museum as part of urban renewal efforts had a 60 percent vacancy rate in 2008.

This did not happen by accident. Some of it was the result of racism. Some of it came out of a natural desire by many Americans to enjoy family life in a new home where conflicts of the sort described here could be avoided. But much of it was the result of a misbegotten public policy. It began with an approach to urban renewal that was comparable to doing brain surgery with a meat axe. In Westcott, for example, no consideration was given to how social capital in the old Fifteenth Ward might be maintained or even strengthened through historic preservation of buildings and more widely dispersed relocation of the neediest residents. The contours of the present neighborhood were decisively cast by housing policies that created a "black township" in Rolling Green Estates, isolating the poorest African-American families from their middle-class neighbors and concentrating them in ways that bred dependency and distrust. Meanwhile, other federal policies encouraged white flight by providing low-interest-rate mortgages and tax breaks for homeowners in the suburbs while redlining many neighborhoods in the city. There were subsidies for exit but a pittance for genuine renewal of the urban infrastructure.

In Syracuse, as in most cities of the northeastern United States, suburbs used their jurisdictional powers to virtually zone out the poor and the black. By 1990 only 1.4 percent of the 305,113 persons living in the Syracuse suburbs were black, and only 4 percent were in families living below the poverty line. In the city, by contrast, 20 percent of the population was black, and 23 percent lived in poverty, including 39 percent of children younger than six. By 2008, more than 70 percent of public school children in Syracuse were poor enough to qualify for subsidized lunches. The suburbs were still less than 2 percent black.

The burden of school desegregation was borne almost entirely by the city, not by the larger metropolitan area. Policies designed to accomplish desegregation in Syracuse may have been more effective than those in many cities of the Northeast (with a higher than average number of schools in racial balance until the 1990s), but they were still crude. It was an urban policy designed by social engineers and lawyers concerned with bus schedules and quotas. The teachers on the frontlines were poorly prepared to deal with the traumas, dislocations, and anger that escalated rapidly on a large scale, pushing many schools beyond the tipping point of civility virtually overnight. While no amount of planning could have avoided the inevitable pain and sense of loss that accompanies any major social change, the outcome would have been vastly different if school desegregation had been a metropolitan rather than a city-only burden.

In the years that I taught at Hamilton High and worked to renew the Westcott neighborhood, I believed you could save cities one school and one neighborhood at a time. I was wrong. We slowed the exodus and even drew some young families to Westcott, but there was a net loss of social capital. Many of those adventurous young couples left for the suburbs when their children reached school age or finished elementary school. We built some bridges across lines of race and class, but today it is a rare white person who dares to walk on the sidewalk bordering Rolling Green Estates. We helped revive the business district, upgraded housing, and made it a better neighborhood in many ways. Caring neighbors continue to look out for one another, cut lawns and carry out the trash for the disabled, drive elders on weekly trips to the supermarket, and look in on the sick. My wife and I have no plans to leave. But despite the real gains we made in Westcott, little that we accomplished was able to touch the underlying problems of increasing poverty, joblessness, and failing schools that afflicted the city as whole. It takes vision and action on a larger scale to change the context within which neighborhood reforms will succeed.

In Raleigh, North Carolina, the seeds of that kind of metropolitan reform were embedded early, right after the Civil War.

3 Three Reconstructions of Raleigh

One of the bloodiest battles of the Civil War was fought south of Raleigh less than a month before Robert E. Lee surrendered to Ulysses S. Grant at Appomattox on April 9, 1865. Confederate General Joseph E. Johnston was traveling north to unite with Lee's army when his troops were crushed at Bentonville, North Carolina, by General William Tecumseh Sherman's forces. Nearly 3,000 Confederate soldiers were killed and wounded. The survivors, some of them barefoot, retreated through Raleigh in what an observer described as "the saddest spectacle of my life."[1]

Though Raleigh's citizens were concerned about the retreating Confederate soldiers, they were mostly fearful that Sherman would destroy their city, the capital of North Carolina. After burning most of Atlanta and conquering Savannah, he had cut a wide path of destruction on his march north through South Carolina toward Raleigh in pursuit of Johnston's army. After the defeat at Bentonville on March 21, Raleigh's mayor and a group of city commissioners set out to meet Sherman as his troops crossed into Wake County and to surrender the city unconditionally. Their assurances to Sherman that he would find no military resistance in Raleigh were nearly upset when a wayward

Confederate lieutenant waited in ambush as Sherman's troops marched up Morgan Street in the rain. When they were only 100 yards distant, the young lieutenant mounted his horse and charged, firing six rounds on the Union troops. As he tried to make a turn at a gallop off Morgan Street, his horse fell and he was captured. The lieutenant's request for time to write a letter to his wife was refused, and he was hanged minutes later near Capitol Square.[2]

After those tense moments, peace reigned and Raleigh, then a city of about 8,000 in a county of 30,000, was saved. Sherman, who had shown so little mercy toward Atlanta, was generous to Raleigh. In fact, the terms he offered to Johnston were so liberal that one northern newspaper said it almost seemed that Sherman had "surrendered" to Johnston rather than the other way around. General Grant, who admired Sherman, went to Raleigh to ask him to renegotiate for the same terms that Lee had recently agreed to. Sherman did, and Johnston complied.[3]

Sherman's army was nearly twice the population of the county, and some plundering occurred despite orders forbidding it. But the army also shared its food with those who had been impoverished by the war, both black and white. Sherman sent guards to Wake Forest College to safeguard its library, and for the most part homes and public buildings were respected. Sherman's aide, Major George Nichols, wrote glowing accounts of Raleigh and its beautiful lawns that "remind one of an English country place." He praised the high proportion of "educated and refined" citizens who exhibited "little of that painful ostentation which is met in Charleston."[4] Major Nichols was speaking about white citizens, of course, though they made up less than half of Raleigh's population at the end of the war. Even Union soldiers did not yet think of blacks as citizens, though a number of free blacks had joined Union ranks.

After the war, some rural blacks in the vicinity of Raleigh who had been treated well by their former owners continued to work for them in exchange for food and wages. Others were turned out from the farms where they had worked, or they left voluntarily, to try their luck in the city. Some free blacks were already making a living in the state capital before the war, and Sherman had little doubt that educated blacks throughout the South would avidly pursue their new rights. He had come to this conclusion in Savannah a few months earlier, during a remarkable "colloquy" with the black leaders of that city.

Sherman's famous March to the Sea had cut the South in two and brought the Confederacy to near-collapse. Thousands of slaves had abandoned plantations in Georgia and South Carolina and followed Sherman's army to Savannah. This unexpected spectacle caused Lincoln's cabinet to turn their attention away from winning the war, to focus on the great questions of what would become known as Reconstruction. What should be done about the four million blacks who had been in bondage? What would freedom mean to former slaves? Were they capable of making decisions for themselves and becoming effective citizens of the United States? Would whites be able to work with them to build an interracial democracy after the end of slavery? Secretary of War Edwin M. Stanton "seemed desirous of coming into contact with the negroes to confer with them," Sherman later recalled, and invited "the most intelligent of the negroes" of Savannah to meet with him on January 12, 1865, at the house where he made his headquarters.

Twenty black leaders came, most of them Baptist and Methodist ministers. While only 5 percent of the nation's black population was free in 1860, eleven of the men who met with Stanton and Sherman had become free before the war ended, either by self-purchase, through the will of a deceased owner, or by birth to a woman who was not enslaved. Although it was against the law to teach slaves to read or write, several of them had learned in secret. One of them, James Porter, an Episcopal vestryman, had operated a clandestine school to teach black children to read. James D. Lynch, who became Mississippi's secretary of state during Reconstruction and earned a reputation as "a great orator, fluid and graceful," was the only black present who had lived in the North before the war. He had attended Kimball Union Academy in New Hampshire and taught school in Jamaica, New York.

Garrison Frazier, a Baptist minister who had purchased his freedom, was the spokesman for the group. Asked to define slavery, he replied that it meant one person's "receiving by irresistible power the work of another man, and not by his consent." He left no doubt that blacks were ready and capable to assume the responsibilities of freedom, which he defined as "placing us where we could reap the fruit of our own labor, and take care of ourselves." Then, summing up what would in fact become one of the central issues of Reconstruction politics, Frazier said this could best be accomplished if blacks had "land, and turn it and till it by our own labor."

Disagreement arose only when Frazier was asked whether blacks would want to live "scattered among whites" or in their own communities. He responded: "I would prefer to live by ourselves, for there is a prejudice against us in the South that will take years to get over." Lynch argued that it would be best to live together, a position that a majority of blacks in America came to adopt. Frazier affirmed the loyalty of all blacks to the Union cause and mentioned that if all the prayers that had been raised in black churches were read out "you would not get through them these two weeks." Turning to Sherman, he said blacks saw him as one "specially set apart by God" to "accomplish the work" of emancipation.[5]

Raleigh's First Reconstruction

Although racists portrayed blacks as corrupt and incompetent during Reconstruction, and sustained that myth for many decades afterward, this remarkable colloquy between Sherman, Stanton, and the black leadership of Savannah was not an isolated event. It was representative of the aspirations and talents of black leadership emerging all across the South. On July 4, 1865, three months after Sherman entered Raleigh, blacks had special reason to celebrate Independence Day. Three thousand jubilant freedmen participated in a "very orderly procession to the grounds of the Peace Institute, where they heard both Negro and white speakers" give thanks for the end of conflict. Both races "partook of an excellent collation, spread on tables."[6] When the party was over, blacks in Raleigh and throughout North Carolina went back to work preparing what became the first statewide black political convention in the South.

They surprised many by being well-enough organized to open their convention in late September, ahead of North Carolina's whites. Representing about half the counties in the state, 117 delegates of the North Carolina Freedmen's Convention met in the Methodist African Church in Raleigh. Among blacks from the city and Wake County who played leading roles in the convention was James H. Harris, later elected to the state legislature. Blacks were still mourning the assassination of Abraham Lincoln on April 14, just five days after the surrender at Appomattox. Although Andrew Johnson, who became president after Lincoln's death, was born in Raleigh, it was a plaster bust of Lincoln that hung over the Freedmen's lectern, inscribed with Lincoln's words "Malice towards none." The Reverend James Walker Burns of New Bern presided, opening the convention with an appeal to "avoid all harsh expressions toward anybody . . . The white people are our neighbors and many of them our friends. We and the white people have got to live together." He counseled blacks to have patience and moderation, "yet assert always we want three things—first, the right to give evidence in the courts; second, the right to be represented in the jury-box; and third, the right to put votes in the ballot box," placing the issue of black suffrage squarely before the convention. Lincoln's Emancipation Proclamation had freed the slaves, but it said nothing about their rights as citizens.

In their appeals for equal rights and equal educational opportunities, the Freedmen's Convention in North Carolina echoed what Sherman had heard in Savannah. It was an extraordinary historical moment—former slaves meeting to offer forgiveness to their former masters while also asserting their rights as free men. The Freedmen's convention adopted the Reverend Burns's address and forwarded it to the all-white Constitutional Convention that met in Raleigh in October, where it was "courteously received" and put aside. The whites' convention concluded that the consequences of slavery "will inevitably affect the state of society for years to come" and that "prejudices of a social character will probably forever exist." The convention went on to draw up a constitution that enabled the North Carolina legislature to adopt the notorious black codes—essentially returning blacks to a state of semislavery. North Carolina's black codes were somewhat more liberal than those adopted in other states of the former Confederacy but did not grant blacks the right to vote or other rights equal to those enjoyed by whites.[7]

The United States Congress, dominated by Republicans who

wanted to assure equal rights for blacks—and more radical members arguing for redistribution of whites' lands to their former slaves—refused to seat whites elected from states with black codes. A crisis ensued over President Johnson's opposition to the radicals' Reconstruction program, and it was not resolved until Johnson was impeached and put on trial in the Senate. In the bargaining that ensued, Johnson's lawyers told the Senate that Johnson would stop obstructing the Congress's Reconstruction policy if he were acquitted. By a margin of one vote, Johnson's impeachment failed and the Republican Reconstruction program went forward. It required southern states to adopt new constitutions and ratify new amendments empowering blacks. But dreams of "40 acres and a mule" were dashed when Congress returned to white owners the land that had been given to blacks by the Freedmen's Bureau at the end of the war.

Reconstruction policy now turned on electoral politics. By 1868, many blacks stood for office and 90 percent of blacks voted throughout the South, helping elect the Republican Ulysses S. Grant as president by a large margin. They ratified new state constitutions providing not only equal rights but also the South's first state-funded schools for both blacks and whites. They elected state legislatures with significant black representation at a time when blacks could vote in only eight states in the North (five New England states—Connecticut was the exception—plus New York, Wisconsin, and Nebraska).[8]

Southern Democrats—virtually all-white—made openly racist appeals against ratification of the new constitutions. In North Carolina, Jonathan Worth complained that the "dregs of society" would become the state's new rulers, making it plain that he was referring to poor whites as well as blacks who would become voters and take office. Despite these efforts, Republicans came to power in North Carolina, as they did in most of the

South. Unlike some Deep South states where blacks constituted a majority of voters, however, North Carolina was only one-fifth black. Coalitions of black and white voters were necessary for Republican victories. Among the thousands of whites who voted with blacks in North Carolina, some were so-called carpetbaggers—northerners, often soldiers, who settled throughout the South after the war, carrying all they had in bags made of carpetlike material. But many more were native white owners of small farms in the western mountainous region of the state who wanted to overthrow the old planter aristocracy and had been sympathetic to the Union cause during the war. The Republican Party also drew some influential native whites in eastern North Carolina, a part of the state that was heavily black. The Democrats labeled them as opportunistic scalawags and traitors who changed party allegiance to gain the spoils of office. It is impossible to weigh the motives of every voter, but many of these whites believed a new social order was possible and wanted to help make it work.[9]

Eric Anderson's careful study of the heavily black second congressional district, which abutted Raleigh and Wake County until it was later redistricted, argued that these Republican whites were courageous in helping to create a truly biracial politics for more than a generation following the Civil War. While whites were sometimes inconsistent, the "awkward yet viable black and white partnership" of North Carolina's Reconstruction era Republican Party "represented the strongest defender of black interests." It was an institution that used politics to settle issues that could have exploded into racial conflict.[10]

North Carolina's biracial politics helped prevent the white terrorism that kept blacks away from polls in Mississippi and other Deep South states in the mid-1870s. Southern "Redeemers" who organized the Ku Klux Klan and other white vigilante groups sought to restore the Old South and reverse the course of Reconstruction. They lynched, shot, beat, and terrorized many blacks. Intimidation of black voters was particularly violent in Mississippi prior to the election of 1875. At a Republican barbecue in Clinton, more than thirty blacks were murdered, some of them schoolteachers and ministers. In some Mississippi counties where black voting had been heavy in 1873, not a single vote was cast by a registered black Republican in 1875. Democrats swept control of the legislature and forced the Republican governor to resign.[11]

But in North Carolina, for more than three decades after the Civil War, white terrorists were unable to gain a foothold. In 1871 a jury impaneled in Raleigh indicted 981 persons for committing Klan violence across the state. In 1898, however, whites went on a rampage in Wilmington and ousted black officeholders. This was the beginning of the end of Reconstruction in North Carolina, yet what is remarkable is that it did not come until more than two decades after Reconstruction ended in most of the South. In order to settle the contested presidential election of 1876, Republican candidate Rutherford B. Hayes agreed to withdraw federal troops from the South and refrain from further intervention in southern affairs. This Compromise of 1877 is cited by most historians as the end of Reconstruction in the South. Soon thereafter, black voters were intimidated and pushed out of office. By 1890, southern states had begun to disenfranchise blacks by passing a variety of laws that virtually eliminated black suffrage in the South.[12]

North Carolina, again, was an exception. Blacks continued to vote and hold office until 1900. Democrats gerrymandered some districts to reduce black majorities in the eastern counties and attacked scalawag whites for supporting "Negro domination" as blacks continued to win elections and gain appointive office.

Politics got meaner and more racist throughout the state as white supremacists gained a stronger hand, but prior to the Wilmington riot in 1898 there was virtually no violent intimidation of black voters.

As the historian Eric Anderson noted, North Carolina was then the only state in the South to "tolerate so great a degree of black participation." Fifteen or more blacks were elected to the statehouse through the 1880s. In 1896, a Fusion ticket of populists, unionist farmers, blacks, and Republican whites took control of the legislature and elected the first Republican governor in twenty years. Eleven blacks went to the statehouse, and George White went to the U.S. House of Representatives. When White was reelected in 1898, he was the only remaining black congressman. A widely respected and persuasive speaker, he pointed out to Democrats that since he was the only black left in Congress, the white cry of "Negro domination" was hollow.[13]

Democrats and some historians hostile to Reconstruction referred to it as a time of "Negro rule." But no black was elected governor of any southern state even at the height of federally enforced Reconstruction. Power remained in white hands at the top echelons of politics. The phrase "Negro rule" had resonance because blacks were elected as sheriffs and county commissioners, they received appointments as postmasters and judges, and they served on juries. More than 300 black magistrates were appointed in the eastern counties of North Carolina, along with dozens of black postmasters. There had always been some degree of private intimacy between household slaves and whites throughout the South, but these appointments brought about a degree of public equality that had never existed. For the first time in the history of the South, whites had daily contacts with African Americans in situations where blacks were in charge.[14]

By the late 1890s, Democratic newspapers in North Carolina,

yearning for a return to white supremacy, played on the emotions stirred up by this reversal of roles. The *Kinston Free Press* mockingly declared it the only state in the Union that still offered the inducements of "citizenship and political honors" to African Americans. It predicted that blacks would swarm to North Carolina: "Let it be proclaimed to the world that the white people of North Carolina have endorsed this Republican policy . . . can anyone doubt that there will be an influx of negroes into North Carolina from Virginia, South Carolina, and other southern states that will soon give the negroes the majority in many counties where they are now in the minority?" Under the headline "Nigger! Nigger! Nigger!" another paper listed all the offices blacks now held. *The New Bern Journal* expressed indignation that a white man might be arrested by a black and forced to go before an African-American magistrate, or to seek a marriage license or the registration of a deed from a black judge.[15]

These editorials, published in 1898, acknowledged that revolutionary social changes had won the support of many white Republicans, although far less than a majority of all whites. Racist customs still dominated life in North Carolina, but a significant shift had occurred in race relations throughout the state and especially in the capital, where black and white legislators mingled. Contrary to later caricatures, blacks elected in North Carolina were mostly responsible—and often distinguished— leaders. Six of the ten blacks serving in the General Assembly in the 1890s had some college education; four of them had bachelor's degrees. A former slave elected to Congress in 1875, John Adams Hyman, was accused of accepting a bribe while serving in the statehouse at Raleigh, but the charge was never proved. James O'Hara, a black Catholic, won praise as a legislator of "vigor and skill." He was a congressman for two terms beginning in 1882 after serving as a clerk in the Treasury Department in Washington, D.C., where he had studied at Howard University. Henry Plummer Cheatham, who went to Congress in 1889, graduated with honors from Raleigh's Shaw University and served as principal of a teacher-training school. A Democratic paper wrote of Cheatham, "If a Republican and a colored man has to succeed [a white] . . . he has our respect and confidence." George White was admired during his three terms in Congress in the 1890s.[16]

Aid programs sponsored by the Freedmen's Bureau had also drawn many blacks to Raleigh. Though short-lived, the bureau had helped to expand schooling and hospitals. Shaw University, founded in 1870 for the education of African Americans, became a magnet for aspiring blacks. While the bureau was prevented from redistributing land, educated blacks became teachers and ministers and began to move out of poverty. Other skilled African Americans became blacksmiths, carpenters, barbers, and bricklayers. Many bought land. In the counties to the east of Raleigh, more than a fifth of blacks moved from sharecropping to farming their own land. Black workers began to bargain for better wages, using the threat of moving to the sugar plantations of Louisiana, where black labor was in high demand at better wages.[17]

The new status of African Americans in Raleigh was evident in more informal ways as well. In the antebellum period, white planters had often invited their slaves to a big summer feast after the crops were planted. Now at political barbecues, blacks freely heckled white speakers who expressed racist views. North Carolina had become "a fascinating mosaic of accommodation between whites and blacks."[18] In more than thirty years since the war—the state's first period of reconstruction—Raleigh had created a discourse across the races that would shape its future in powerful ways in the twentieth century, despite severe setbacks.

But by the end of the nineteenth century, white supremacists had finally won the political battle in North Carolina. Ironically, in 1896, when the Fusionists triumphed at the polls, the United States Supreme Court issued its infamous decision in *Plessy v. Ferguson*, ruling that enforced separation of blacks from whites on railroad cars did not violate the constitutional rights of African Americans. The Court's majority opinion confirmed the supremacist ideology: "Legislation is powerless to eradicate racial distinctions based on physical differences . . . If one race be inferior to the other socially, the Constitution of the United States cannot put them on the same plane." North Carolina Democrats ran a blatant white-supremacy campaign in 1898, and their victory was, they claimed, a rejection of black political power as fostered by the Fusionists. The headline in the Raleigh *News and Observer* summed it up: "White Men Will Rule." In 1898 the Supreme Court approved the disenfranchisement laws that had been adopted earlier in Mississippi. By 1900 North Carolina had disenfranchised nearly all black voters in the state.[19]

Saying "I cannot live in North Carolina and be a man," George White announced he would not seek reelection to Congress.[20] But the kind of white supremacy that finally triumphed in North Carolina was not restricted to the South. Disenfranchisement of blacks was a keystone of what the historian C. Vann Woodward called "the permission to hate"—a sentiment that found support not in only in Supreme Court decisions but also among northerners eager to appease the South and embrace "imperialistic adventures and aggression against colored peoples in distant lands" from the Philippines and Hawaii to nearby Cuba.[21]

Raleigh's Second Reconstruction

In a meeting with 88 other black leaders, George White urged them to threaten large-scale emigration to stop the disenfranchisement plan. But White's proposal was narrowly defeated. He left North Carolina, saying that the disenfranchisement was not just political emasculation but the beginning of a "general degradation of the negro." White correctly foresaw the Jim Crow culture that would spread across the South. The phrase refers to laws that went beyond the black codes that Reconstruction had struck down. After regaining control of the ballot box, whites passed legislation that not only separated blacks in railroad cars but specified where they could and could not eat, drink, sleep, and go to school. "White only" signs appeared in waiting rooms in bus stations as well as over drinking fountains and entrances to public toilets. In the Negro State Fair held in Raleigh in 1901, the newly inaugurated governor, Charles B. Aycock, told assembled blacks: "The law that separates you from the white people of the state socially always has been and always will be inexorable . . . it is absolutely necessary that the [black] race have a society of its own."[22]

Some blacks emigrated north with George White but most reluctantly settled into the only world they knew, accepting Booker T. Washington's advice "that the agitation of questions of social equality is the extremist folly." As president of the Tuskegee Institute in Alabama, Washington preached that patience and industrial education would provide economic independence and self-respect for his fellow African Americans while they waited for better days. Most also felt the stinging truth of what W. E. B. Du Bois wrote in *Black Reconstruction in America:* "The slave went free; stood a brief moment in the sun; and then moved back again toward slavery."[23] Lynchings of black men and women reached a national peak in 1919, when 70 African Americans were hanged. By the mid-1920s, the Ku Klux Klan had more than five million members, a majority of them outside the South.

Black businesses in Raleigh were forced off of Fayetteville Avenue, the city's main street, and into a separate black district, as white owners of commercial property refused to rent to blacks. But Raleigh experienced little violence and no lynching. Although black businesses were segregated, whites in Raleigh refused to adopt laws enforcing residential segregation, as the cities of Greensboro and Winston-Salem had done in specifying white blocks and black blocks. Though blacks were most heavily concentrated on the southeast side, they continued to be dispersed throughout the city, and racially mixed blocks were not unusual.

Blacks and whites who worked together and sat side-by-side in the same truck nevertheless used separate water fountains and separate entrances to theaters. Occasionally, the dominant pattern was reversed, with whites sitting in the balcony of black theaters when leading black bands came to town. The subtleties of racial interaction were revealed when the Raleigh *News and Observer* criticized a University of North Carolina professor for accepting an invitation to dinner with James. W. Ford, the black Communist Party candidate for vice president of the United States in 1936. Ford had drawn a sizable crowd, many of them white students, to his rally. The *News and Observer* editorialist did not criticize the professor, E. E. Ericson, for attending an interracial event, even a Communist rally, but for sitting down to dinner afterward with black people. This constituted "a gratuitous gesture of defiance toward deep, impregnable and desirable convictions of the people whom the University of North Carolina is established to serve."[24]

The incident also highlighted the progressive sentiments of a significant number of Raleigh whites. Edwin McNeill Poteat Jr., minister at Pullen Memorial Baptist Church, claimed the newspaper's treatment of Ericson undermined its reputation for liberalism: "By stating that the solution of the race problem is the complete separation of the white and Negro people, you have said in effect that you believe in the continued brutal exploitation of the Negro people." Poteat went on to mock the editorialist's defense of racial integrity. "The fact is that racial integrity is not impaired by men like Ericson eating with Negro men. It is impaired by men, not like Ericson, sleeping with Negro women." A graduate student who had taken a class with Ericson dismissed the newspaper's charge that the professor had attended the interracial dinner to flout southern custom, noting that no one seeking publicity would have asked that reporters not be invited to the dinner. Perhaps it was Professor Ericson's humility in eating with African Americans that angered other whites, the student suggested.[25]

Raleigh's two black institutions of higher education, Shaw University and St. Augustine College, continued to draw talent to Raleigh. Government employment in the state capital also helped to support an articulate, if still segregated, black middle class. The first relaxation of the color line came in the 1930s when the reading room in the state library was silently desegregated. In 1932 fifteen African-American leaders were elected to the Raleigh Citizens Committee, whose stated aims were securing civil rights and economic advancement for black people. By the 1940s, as southern blacks—including about a fourth of Wake County's African-American population—flooded to northern cities, progressive whites and blacks in Raleigh began to meet to discuss possibilities for further racial integration.[26]

During World War II, white and black women in Raleigh met separately to roll surgical bandages for the troops. But the war became a turning point in the expectations held by blacks. A majority of African Americans who responded to a poll by *Carolina Times* said the effort to attain equal treatment should be pushed, including legal action to equalize the schools even while the war continued. President Harry Truman's 1948 executive orders to end discrimination in federal employment and in the military had a great effect throughout the nation and a momentous impact especially in the South, where many military bases were located. Truman's order, which affected both enlisted personnel and civilian employees, integrated living quarters as well as schools, clubs, and swimming pools on military bases.

Meanwhile, the National Association for the Advanced of Colored People began to bring cases to the Supreme Court to end school desegregation, beginning with university professional schools. The University of North Carolina admitted the first black student to its medical school in 1951. In Raleigh, the president of the local chapter of the NAACP, Ralph Campbell, brought black leaders together to plan desegregation strategies in what became known as the "oval table" group, referring to the shape of Campbell's dining room table.

School facilities for African-American students were improved and per pupil expenditures in black and white schools were nearly equalized in Raleigh prior to the Supreme Court's 1954 *Brown v. Board of Education* decision declaring separate schools unconstitutional. There was no massive resistance to desegregation in North Carolina—the state did not close schools under threats of violence or issue tuition vouchers so that students could attend private white academies, as did Virginia, for example. What did happen, as Jack Michael McElreath showed in his history of the period, could be described as genteel resistance or clever obstruction.

North Carolina's legislature acted quickly to pass the Pearson Plan, which gave all authority for racial assignment to local schools and provided that any appeal be made to the state courts. The parents of a ninth grader, Joseph Holt Jr., brought the first case in 1956. They wanted Joseph to attend a white school only a few blocks from their Oberlin Road residence rather than walk nearly four miles to a black school. The school superintendent offered free transportation for Holt and other blacks on Oberlin Road if the parents would withdraw their request. They accepted the compromise for that year and reapplied for transfer to a white school for the next three years but were turned away by an unsympathetic board and state courts. Holt's father was fired from his job as a shipping clerk. The Catholic bishop of Raleigh had desegregated Catholic schools in 1953, but it was not until 1960 that the first black child, William Campbell (son of Ralph Campbell) became the first black admitted to a white public school in Raleigh. While a coalition of liberal white groups joined blacks to press the School Board for faster action, only token school desegregation prevailed for more than a decade after the *Brown* decision.[27]

Attacks on Jim Crow practices outside the schools were more successful. The first move was a model of southern courtesy. In 1959 a group of black students at Shaw University decided to visit white churches in Raleigh. The faculty adviser of the Baptists Student Union sent letters to the Raleigh ministers advising them that only two or three students would visit each church: "This is an effort to get acquainted with the church as it is represented in this city. We hope we will be welcome. We don't want to embarrass anyone."

A year later, only a few days after a highly publicized sit-in at a segregated lunch counter in Greensboro, North Carolina, 150 students from Shaw and St. Augustine colleges sat-in at eight lunch counters in Raleigh. After students were arrested at the upscale Cameron Village shopping center, 59 Raleigh ministers, 46 of whom were white, supported the students and admitted their own complicity in segregative practices: "We speak in penitence for our own failures . . . For us this matter is not primarily one of social custom but one of allegiance to God's Word . . . We confess that the problems of discrimination within our own churches have not been solved." The ministers went on to commend the students for conducting an orderly and nonviolent campaign and called on the citizens of Raleigh "to be fair-minded —to make the name of Raleigh appreciated for its good human relations and friendliness."[28]

This "second reconstruction" was indeed a historic shift from the first one. As John Patrick Daly showed in his brilliant study of southern evangelicalism, white ministers of all denominations wrote impassioned proslavery tracts at the time of the Civil War out of the sincere belief that defending slavery "as a peculiar institution sanctioned by God's Word" was part of their calling to save heathen Africans. Even after the war, most ministers did not interpret defeat of the Confederacy as a rebuke from the Almighty. Rather than condemning the "peculiar institution" of slavery, they lamented that the churches had failed to work diligently in the right spirit to carry out their true mission of saving black souls.[29]

In April 1960, black college students from across the South came to a conference at Shaw and took the first steps toward the founding of what became the Student Nonviolent Coordinating Committee (SNCC, pronounced "snick"). Martin Luther King Jr. spoke to the students, urging them to keep protesting the segregation of lunch counters and other facilities even if that meant many of them would go to jail. He applauded their nonviolent approach, reminding them that the final goal was not defeat of one's opponents but reconciliation with them. In the end, the moral weight of nonviolent protest would "place pressures on the federal government that will compel its intervention."[30]

By summer's end Raleigh's lunch counters had been desegregated. But the protesters continued, widening their focus to discrimination in employment and public facilities. By 1962 the city's swimming pools admitted blacks and whites. After another wave of protests and mass arrests in 1963, Mayor William G. Enloe appointed a biracial committee of 100 to solve the crisis and to "avoid another Birmingham," referring to the violence that broke out in Alabama and the worldwide media coverage that ensued. Enloe also asked John Winters, a black member of the City Council, for advice at a public meeting. Winters replied, "It's hard for you all to understand what these kids are fighting for but you could if they were white." At the end of several weeks of negotiation, 76 Raleigh businesses, the Chamber of Commerce, and the Raleigh Merchants Bureau agreed to a "joint citywide removal of all policies that deny rights and services because of race."[31]

Despite progress on many fronts, by 1965 only 1 percent of Raleigh's black students attended formerly white schools. North Carolina's Deputy Attorney General Ralph Moody warned that the 1964 Civil Rights Acts would allow for no further delay: "No forms of token compliance, clever schemes, chicanery or subtle or sophisticated plans of avoidance—no matter how crafty or cunning—will in the end prevail." In the end, the threat that federal funds would be cut off to noncompliant school districts brought major integration of Raleigh public schools by the end of the decade and completed the second reconstruction of Raleigh. It was not possible to eradicate all vestiges of racism in Raleigh, any more than in Syracuse. But Jim Crow laws had been repealed, and the rules of social interaction had been rewritten. Moreover, a confession of wrongdoing had been made, and not only by ministers.[32] A heavy burden had been lifted from the hearts and minds of many white people in the city, and new energies had been released that would reshape not just schools and lunch counters but also new highways and the physical city as well.

Raleigh's Third Reconstruction

Questions of race were not pushed off the public agenda in North Carolina. On the contrary, Raleigh undertook a third reconstruction that involved a voluntary merger of its public schools with those in the surrounding suburbs. Conversations about merger had been under consideration since 1962 when the Raleigh and Wake County school boards asked the state's planning division to assess the impact of merging. A 1965 study by scholars from Vanderbilt University concluded that merger not only made sense financially and was the best hope for stabilizing long-term racial integration but also "would be a determining factor in the successful development of the Raleigh Wake County Community into a major North Carolina industrial urban complex."[33] But voters rejected a crucial bond issue that would have allowed the first steps to be taken. As Raleigh moved beyond token integration, worries about white flight rose. A 1968 editorial in the Raleigh *News and Observer* raised the possibility that Raleigh might become a "little Chicago . . . with hostile black consciousness and separatism growing with resegregation."[34] Between 1968 and 1976, the year the merger went into effect, the white population of Raleigh dropped 11 percent.

The road to merger was rocky. Anti-busing sentiment was strong. More than 3,000 people filled Raleigh's Memorial Auditorium in 1971 to discuss a plan to further integrate county schools. One speaker who said he supported busing his children "whatever distances necessary to ensure quality education" was loudly booed. Cheers greeted a black parent who said, "Busing 30 miles out of the way is not equality, it's stupidity."[35] A nonbinding referendum on merger was defeated by a 2–1 margin a year later. But pro-merger forces did not give up. Paul Jervay, the black publisher of *The Carolinian,* noted that there were plenty of disagreements during more than a decade of cross-racial dialogue leading up to the merger, as there had been in Raleigh during the period of biracial politics in the first reconstruction after the Civil War: "Folks were fighting tooth and nail against merger, but they fought well and it was an open fight. It was not one of those things where we went into a back room and made a decision and forced it down your throat. It was in your face, and we kept going back and forth. This happened over a period of years. But we kept meeting and kept talking."[36]

A coalition of business, civic, and political leaders of both races grew more concerned as Raleigh's classrooms began to empty and the system moved slowly toward higher concentrations of poor and black pupils. Wake County, fearful of losing its own tax base, had stopped ceding property to the city. According to Robert Farmer, a Wake County delegate to the state legislature, the Raleigh business community decided to support the merger in the end because "the tax base was decaying and property values were going down in the inner city. Business folks didn't want downtown Raleigh to rot."[37]

Among blacks in the coalition, a key concern was to prevent Raleigh from becoming another Durham, a predominantly black and poor school district where test scores were falling. Black political elites in Durham had turned against merger in order to gain control of the school system. Vernon Malone, who became the first black chairman of the merged school board in Wake County, said Raleigh blacks struggled over that question but in the end "most of us were not naive enough to believe that there was glory" in taking command of a school system that would be impoverished by white flight. "It would leave us with control [but] without the financial resources that a countywide tax base would provide."[38]

Smart politics along with years of cross-racial dialogue finally brought the merger about. Still, there were a few hurdles to overcome. While the Raleigh School Board favored merger, the Wake County School Board that governed all the suburban districts was split. The pro-merger coalition helped to elect three new members who favored merger to an expanded countywide school board in 1974. The Wake County delegation to the state legislature followed up by securing passage of a law enabling merger. Both city and county school boards then voted in its favor. A popular referendum was not required. City and suburban children began attending schools in the unified system in 1976. The third reconstruction of Raleigh was under way. In neighboring Durham, by the time the school boards finally voted for merger in 1992, its city schools were 91 percent black.

4   There Are No Bad Schools in Raleigh

On my way to Raleigh in 2003, driving down I-81 past Frackville and Mahanoy in a Pennsylvania blizzard, I wondered if all the hype about the extraordinary success of Raleigh's public schools could be true. While reformers could tell stirring stories of high achievement in a particular urban school here or there, usually attributed to a charismatic principal, Raleigh had transformed an entire urban system in ways that dramatically raised the achievement of poor and minority students in *all* its schools. I had departed that morning from Syracuse, where only 25 percent of eighth graders passed state achievement tests in math and reading. In Raleigh, where city and suburbs had merged to form a single countywide school system that served children of all social classes and races, 91 percent passed.[1]

Astonishingly, because children in the urban core of most of America have become Ralph Ellison's "invisible" children, there had been no outcry in Syracuse, not even at one middle school where 95 percent failed the state math test. In the affluent Syracuse suburb of Fayetteville-Manlius, where only 16 percent did not pass, mass protests would have broken out if even half of the students had failed the state tests, never mind 95 percent.

Enraged parents would have stormed the school headquarters demanding the ouster of the entire School Board. Similar city-suburban gaps can be found in most cities.

But the word "gap" papers over the dangerous reality that these statistics reveal—the failure to make good on an implicit bargain that America made with its poorest citizens. This bargain promised that the great income inequalities permitted in a capitalist society would be balanced by equal educational opportunities for all. The Wake County Public School System, of which Raleigh is a part, is one of the few urban school systems in America that made good on that democratic bargain.[2] Gaps in educational achievement became not only intolerable but unthinkable there. Educators didn't just talk equal educational opportunity. They delivered it to all children in the system, day after day. And they reduced the gap between rich and poor, black and white, more than any other large urban educational system in America.

In the ensuing years, in visits to more than a score of Raleigh schools, I often heard teachers and principals say, "There are no bad schools in Wake County." And they were right. Perhaps the most convincing proof of that lay not just in the stunning test scores across the whole county but in the fact that virtually all the teachers in each school I visited enrolled their own children in Wake County's public schools, most often in the same school where they taught. In Syracuse, it was rare to find teachers who sent their own children to Syracuse public schools. Most teachers with families lived in the suburbs and sent their children to affluent, predominantly white suburban schools. Like the rest of the middle class, they had abandoned the city and its schools long ago.

One of the schools I first visited in Raleigh, Bugg Elementary, lay in the southeast quadrant of the city, which was the historic black district. Although nearly a third of the Bugg children were low income and the school was still majority black—54 percent—it was a magnet school that attracted whites from across the county to its programs in art and science. In third grade 94 percent of white children and 79 percent of blacks passed the state math test. By fifth grade 100 percent of both blacks and whites passed the test. Not all of Bugg's white children were bused to school. Some walked. In a city where housing costs had soared as fast as Syracuse homes had depreciated, the modest ranch houses with neat lawns in the Bugg neighborhood were still a bargain in 2003, and the school's reputation drew white families as well as black ones to buy homes there.

Mary Page, principal of the Bugg School, spread out a large leather briefing book on her desk and gave me a mournful smile when she told me that it wasn't easy to move back to North Carolina. She had attended black segregated schools in the 1950s in Rockingham, a small town in the western part of the state where the movie house was not only segregated but had no toilets for blacks. Her life took a different course at Warren Wilson College, a Presbyterian school near Asheville, where she was one of only seven African-American students in her class. She later went to Germany with her husband, who was serving in the United States Army, and taught there, before settling down as a teacher in northern Virginia's Prince William County. She was not eager to return to North Carolina in 1997 when her husband accepted an offer to be registrar at Shaw University. Her memories of segregation in the rural south had left scars, and she had never lived in Raleigh nor heard much about the success its schools had achieved since the merger with Wake County. She arrived a year before the Wake County system announced that its goal was to have 95 percent of all K–8 students pass state exams in reading and math within five years.

"I thought it was a good goal. I believe you've got to set goals really high. If we had said 80 percent we wouldn't have gotten any more than that." But many thought it was a mistake—that Wake County could not possibly succeed and would wind up with egg on its face. Even Mary Page had doubts. Her first job was vice principal of a school across the street from a large housing project in downtown Raleigh: "To be honest, we had some children whose scores were so low and I thought, my God, how are we going to get those children there."[3] The details of how they got there, or nearly got there with 91.3 percent of all children in Raleigh and Wake County passing state tests five years later, make up one of the most inspiring stories in public education.

Wake County set its goal in 1998 while Bill Clinton was still president and before there was a No Child Left Behind law. But as the nation has discovered, just saying or legislating that no child will be left behind doesn't lift all children or provide equal educational opportunity. It wasn't just setting the goal but transforming the whole educational system over three decades that led to Raleigh's extraordinary success. Change had to reach deep into the schools, touching every family and marshalling community forces in new ways. It had taken political courage to tear down the wall that separated Raleigh's urban schoolchildren from those in the suburbs and rural towns of Wake County, courage that suburbanites in Syracuse had never mustered. In the same decade that Raleigh was making its historic decision in favor of equal educational opportunities, suburban Syracuse refused to even consider a much more modest proposal for voluntary busing of poor black children to some of its more affluent schools. The challenge of making the Raleigh merger work was huge. Nearly everyone I spoke with advised me to start unraveling the tale by talking with Robert Bridges.

Making Merger Work

Bridges had not started out to be a teacher and never dreamed he would become the first black superintendent of Wake County's majority-white school district. His earliest goal was to play basketball for Duke. But blacks from the rural South didn't play for Duke in the mid-1950s, and so he had to settle for Voorhees Junior College in Denmark, South Carolina. Now over 70, and still as trim as an athlete, he moved with the assurance of a Duke player as he ushered me into his house and rearranged the chairs so we could talk.

When he began teaching sixth grade in 1961 in the still segregated Washington Elementary School in downtown Raleigh, Bridges knew he had to be on his toes because Washington's teachers were proud of their school. As a new recruit, now with a bachelor's degree from St. Augustine College, he was told, "'There's a lot expected of you.' We all knew that. We were collegial in the closest sense. There was a sense of pride about what we did. We self-policed. If there was a bad teacher someplace, especially if they had abusive tendencies, it would not be unusual for that person to get identified within the ranks, by the ranks. And either you get it together or, you know, somebody gets you out of there."

High levels of competence were not as common in rural black schools, and even in Raleigh black students dropped out of school in high numbers because so few jobs requiring a high school diploma were open to them. Bridges harbored no nostalgia for segregation, but he wanted me to know that the sense of community in black schools was a precious thing. "Black parents really felt ownership" and had strong bonds with black teachers who had to "figure out what was needed to educate your child and making sure that these things happened. And the most comfortable and most secure place to do that was in the schoolhouse." Black students who did their homework and shined in class were not put down for "acting white," a phenomenon that became so widespread later in racially integrated schools that not only scholars like the anthropologist John Ogbu spoke out against it but also Bill Cosby and Barack Obama.

Raleigh effectively maintained racially separate schools until the late 1960s. Major integration did not come until the Supreme Court's 1971 *Swann* decision approved massive busing in the Charlotte-Mecklenburg school district. But by 1968 Raleigh had already begun to integrate teaching staffs, and a few token black students were admitted to white schools. As a new principal, Bridges winced when the white leaders of the district cherry-picked the black schools for their strongest teachers: "They went into the black schools and deliberately identified the most outstanding teachers we had, by any measure you could use. They gave us some of the sorriest whites—the discards, the malcontents, and the low-performers." What bothered him even more was that black children were getting lost in predominantly white schools where they could no longer rely on the same level of caring or expectations they had experienced in their formerly black schools—not at all unlike what happened in Syracuse schools at that time. Later, the presence of a strong core of able black teachers and principals became a major factor in making integrated schools work.

Whites began to bail out of the system in the 1970s, as they did in Syracuse and elsewhere. The line dividing the inner-city schools from the growing suburbs "had been frozen by the county. So we were just being strangled, dying on the vine," according to Bridges. "We were locked into the inner city. The black count in the Raleigh schools was approaching 40 percent."

But in 1976, without any court order, the Raleigh city and county schools merged to create the Wake County School System. Raleigh had the advantage of being able to merge with a single suburban school system rather than a number of independent school districts, as was the situation in Syracuse and most northern cities.

While merger was a huge step, the transformation of the schools that followed was even more remarkable. Significant racial integration took place in the first years, but the turning point came in 1981 with the appointment of Superintendent Walter Marks, who arrived when the Wake County population was just beginning to explode. In the 1980s the county grew by 41 percent, from 301,000 to 426,000 people. Marks wanted to make sure that growth did not create a second ring of affluent white schools. To keep the district integrated, he needed to expand two-way busing—that is, more whites would have to travel to formerly black schools, while more blacks were bused to predominantly white schools. In order to make busing an attractive alternative, he turned 27 schools into magnet schools in one year—schools with distinctive programs that any parent in the city could choose. That meant transforming the curricula in more than a third of the schools in Wake County.

Bridges, like nearly everyone else, was astonished by Marks's plan. Marks called Bridges to his office within a few weeks of his arrival and appointed him deputy superintendent. "I tried to discourage him. Urged him to start with 10," Bridges recalled. "I was worried about how it was going to affect black kids and Marks said 'Have you got a week?' He took me to Montclair where he had been in charge of magnet schools, and I left there convinced black kids had thrived. Marks was certain that with the right mix of magnet schools we could fill Raleigh's vacant

97

inner city schools with whites from beyond the Beltline, and we did." In turn, magnets in the suburbs drew blacks out of their own "comfort zone" in the city.

As deputy superintendent, Bridges ran day-to-day business for the next year while Marks relentlessly reached out to black and whites in schools, churches, and "living room dialogues" all over Wake County. "He did it every day, morning to night, and was one of the most effective salesmen I ever saw," Bridges recalled. "We had a packed gym one night at an elementary school in the northern part of the county that was overflowing with kids— classrooms in trailers all over the school grounds. Marks laid out his pitch, explaining how exciting these magnet schools were going to be and promising there was no way you would not want your child bused to one of these magnets given all the educational advantages they would offer."

After Marks wrapped up, Bridges went on, "a big red-faced muscular fellow walked halfway to the stage and said, 'We're not having any of this. You've just been hired here. We live here. And we're not going on any buses to anywhere. We want you to build some schools here where we live.' Marks came down with the mike in his hand to meet this guy, who towered over him, and told him, 'There's no money to build schools out here and until you go downtown and fill up those schools you will be in crowded conditions out here. Or you can come downtown and then we can break things loose and do what we need to do.'"

The upshot a year later was that parents from that elementary school and across Wake County applied in such great numbers that all 27 magnet schools were filled and racially balanced. Many had waiting lists. No downtown schools were closed. Marks spent millions upgrading the schools. He created a class of master principals and appointed them to head the new magnets. Some schools developed special programs in the arts and theater, or science and technology. Others established options like the International Baccalaureate diploma. He told teachers he wanted them to stay at a given school only if they truly believed in the new program. In some schools, more than a fourth of the teachers transferred out to more traditional schools in other school districts. He was then able to hire scores of creative teachers who had excelled in magnet schools elsewhere. Once the schools opened, he became legendary for quickly responding to any need teachers had. If they required new pottery kilns, his aides made calls and got them delivered the next day, even if they had to be shipped from Georgia.

Bridges succeeded Marks as county school superintendent and continued to build magnet schools through the 1980s. They remain the heart of Wake County's appeal. In 2006 nearly 50 of the system's 122 schools serving 128,000 students were schools of choice. They were also a testing ground for what works and what doesn't. Programs that failed to draw students were closed down. Programs that thrived and produced results were adapted to other schools. Giving parents a wide range of choices did not mean they always got their first pick, but it enabled Wake County to create what Bridges called "a workable balance in the race and class count" in all its schools. That balance was the major reason there were no bad schools in his county, Bridges believed. "And that's a powerful factor in the kind of expectations you set in the school and the kind of teachers you attract."

While the network of magnet schools laid the right foundation and test scores rose, improvement was slow for the bottom third of students. In 1994 state tests showed that nearly 30 percent of Wake County's third graders failed math and reading. Karen Banks, a spunky woman who came from Texas to head a new department of evaluation, said the system had grown too fast and had too many diffuse goals in the early 1990s. Wake had three superintendents after Bridges left, but the man she credited with taking the school system to the next level was Bill McNeal, who became the county's second black superintendent. As deputy superintendent for instruction, McNeal had urged Wake's School Board to adopt its own No Child Left Behind policy in 1998 when George W. Bush was still governor of Texas.

McNeal's bold proposal had deep personal roots. He knew in his bones that all children could learn and graduate from high school. He grew up in Durham, where his father worked at the lowliest jobs in the Liggett and Myers tobacco factory, in part because he didn't know how to read or write. His mother had stood for grueling days on the assembly line of a poultry plant. Yet all four of their children graduated from college. McNeal remembered that his father taught himself to read by watching an early morning public television program. He later earned a high school diploma after years in night school and went on to become a Baptist minister while still working days at Liggett and Myers. He preached at two churches every Sunday and died at the age of 91.

McNeal helped the family by working summers in the tobacco fields. He earned his college tuition for North Carolina Central University by doing the night shift at Shoney's restaurant, from 5 p.m. to 1:30 a.m. He started as a bus boy and was eventually given the key to the store so that he could fulfill the duties of assistant manager, though he was never given the title. A patronizing Shoney's supervisor told him that when he finished college they would make him manager. "I was already training whites with only high school degrees to become managers," McNeal recalled. "I had no intention of coming back."

In the 1960s he lost his draft deferment when he dropped out of college to earn more money to help out his sister. But he was not sent to Vietnam. After getting the second highest test scores in his battalion at boot camp, he was picked to train as an instructor. That experience shaped his beliefs that even those with the poorest educational opportunities could learn. It also convinced him to get certified as a teacher when he returned to North Carolina Central University.

His first job after college took him to a large desegregated high school in Connecticut, where he taught social studies and was appointed advisor of the Afro-American Club, as it was then called. About 250 of the 3,000 students in the school were black. He had been there only four months when serious racial issues started to unfold. McNeal went to the principal to tell him the place was about to come apart: "I know the kids are upset. They feel they are not getting the best classes. They think they are mistreated in the halls, and they believe there are double standards when they are in the classrooms. You need to spend some time listening to them."

The principal said he would but continued to rely on McNeal as his conduit and never met with the students. A month later a full-scale riot broke out and the National Guard had to be called in. The principal was replaced. McNeal helped the new principal work through the issues with black and white students, and then decided to return to North Carolina. He had learned that you can't isolate people because "the more isolated those black students were the angrier they became." It could happen not only in a desegregated school system but also in a single classroom. Real integration of different kinds of people "means that I now start to understand who you are and what you are about."

Raleigh hired him to teach eighth grade American history at Carroll Middle School, which even in 1974 was very diverse. He saw anew that teaching was all about relationships. "I found that when you put a hand on a shoulder you will get to know them as a person. You need to get to know their family members, too.

It pays huge dividends down the road." He asked each of his students to write a small book, *The Little Government that Grew*, to tell the story of the founding and growth of America and how major changes came about. The year-long project ended with each child teaching his or her book to a third grader in a nearby school. He coached them not to read it but to teach it so a third grader could understand it. "To do that they really needed to understand it themselves." He also wanted them to develop self-confidence as speakers and storytellers. McNeal went with his students when they gave their lessons so that he could compliment and critique their teaching.

The Afro haircut that McNeal wore in the 1970s was long gone, but he still held fast to the beliefs he developed back then about how to reach all children: "Bottom line: When they cross that threshold, the expectation is that you will educate them. If not, I want to know why."

Setting the 95 Percent Goal

Wake County set the goal of having 95 percent of all K–8 students achieve at or above grade level by 2003. The goal would be measured by state tests in grades 3 through 8. Karen Banks, the new director of evaluation, rejoiced at having a single, focused goal. On the day the School Board met to vote, she doubted that anyone in the room realized the galvanizing effect the goal would have. "Many people thought we were crazy," Banks said. "There were concerns that teachers would not support the goal because it was unrealistic and that we would have a backlash from parents of high-achieving children who thought they would be shortchanged." A high official in the North Carolina State Department of Education warned her that Wake was creating expectations it couldn't possibly fulfill: "Karen, why did you let them set that 95 percent goal? You all aren't going to be able to reach that high of a goal in five years."

Within the Wake County school system, however, McNeal had begun a revolution years earlier to prepare the principals and top staff for the change. That was why Banks's contribution was so important: she moved the system to data-driven thinking with her creative analyses of what worked and what did not. McNeal's own conversion had come in 1989 when he attended a workshop with Edward Deming, the organizational guru whose theories the Japanese credited for their economic miracle. McNeal arranged seminars so that his top staff could interact with Deming to learn how to analyze data to intervene more quickly and speed up change. He also made sure that principals could understand and effectively use the new data Banks's office was producing to reallocate resources within their schools. McNeal did not use the word "fired," but in one year he "moved" 27 principals who were failing to act aggressively enough to develop plans to reach low-performing children.

When he was named superintendent, McNeal linked his own contract renewal and salary increments to success in reaching the 95 percent goal. "I got some calls from friends of mine in the black community," he said. "I followed two white superintendents who had received good raises whether scores went up or not. My friends were asking, 'Oh my God, is this what a black man has to do to get the top job now?'" He told them the salary plan was his own idea: "Should the Board expect me to close the academic achievement gap of students in the district? Absolutely. Can they quantify that? Absolutely. Should they expect me to recruit the best and retain the brightest? Absolutely. That's my job." McNeal understood what he was doing in setting a standard for his own performance, and felt it was one of the best things he ever did. He intended to send a message: "I wanted the whole community to own this goal and I wanted to start by showing my commitment to it."

Unlike Bush's policy, which was underfunded and left millions of children behind in high-poverty inner-city schools, Wake County has come close to its educational goal under McNeal. Not every school attained a 95 percent passing rate, but many did. While only 71 percent of third graders passed the state's math and reading tests in 1994, by 2003 more than 91 percent of all Wake students in grades 3 through 8 had done so. McNeal was named National Superintendent of the Year in 2004 by the Association of American School Administrators.

At the same time, the test score gap between black and white children shrank dramatically. When the 95 percent goal was set, only 57 percent of black children in grades 3 through 8 were passing the state math test. By 2003, 81 percent passed. White scores also rose, but the gap between whites and blacks had shrunk from 37 points to 17. The gap between Hispanic students and whites narrowed from 28 points to 11. The passing rate for poor children, defined as those with family incomes low enough to qualify for free or reduced-price lunch, rose from 55 to 80 percent in the same period.

Some have suggested that much of Wake's school achievement was a result of the economic boom Raleigh enjoyed, drawing wealthier and more education-conscious parents to its schools. But the data show that the percentage of students categorized as impoverished or minority population increased after the goal was set, due in part to large immigration of Hispanic students into the Raleigh-Durham area. Poor students in elementary schools rose from 10 to 15 percent, and minority students rose from 31 to 43 percent. The system as a whole became 40 percent minority and 27 percent African American. If Syracuse had chosen merger at the same time that Raleigh did, it would have had less of an integration problem, since only 9 percent of the metropolitan population was black and only 13 percent was impoverished. In 2006 Wake County's per pupil expenditure was slightly below the mean for comparable school systems, and it was several thousand dollars less than Syracuse provided per pupil.

Some critics have suggested that perhaps North Carolina's state exams were just not as difficult as those of New York and other northern states. But Wake County students performed well in national comparisons as well. In 1990, with less than half of Wake's seniors—most of them college-bound—taking the SAT, the county scored below the national average. Yet in 2007, with 76 percent of Wake's high school seniors taking the test (compared with a national average participation rate of 48 percent), the average score of 1057 was 40 points above the national average. Wake students scored 11 points higher than the national average on the SAT writing test that was introduced in 2006. Wake's improved scores on state tests reflect the kinds of gains in mathematical reasoning and verbal skill that national tests measure and colleges value.

How, then, did Wake do it? Was it just setting a goal and using increased testing to whip teachers and students until they met the new target? Superintendent McNeal agreed with Bridges on the principal reason. Breaking down the wall between affluent suburbs and impoverished inner cities created a "healthy balance" of rich and poor in every classroom. And in 2000, Wake was the first metropolitan school district to move away from racial balance to economic balance as the measure of a school's diversity. Any school in Wake County where more than 40 percent of pupils were poor enough to qualify for subsidized lunches was defined as being out of balance. The policy guaranteed that all schools in Wake County would have a core of middle-class students who would establish a floor of positive expectations and create student networks across class lines that would benefit poor students.[4] Through this network of friends, less privileged students would get to know parents who might help them get a job or gain admission to college or simply serve as role models. Schools with a majority of middle-class parents will not tolerate incompetent teachers, or drinking fountains that don't work, or restrooms with no toilet paper.

Wake had begun to move to a class-based definition of diversity in the late 1990s, when its board reviewed research showing the strong link between family income and achievement— namely, that the achievement of children was depressed in schools with high concentrations of poverty. It began to use socioeconomic status as one of the three key factors in its assignment policy. The other two were racial diversity and pupil achievement level. The board had also become sensitized to court rulings in the South that prohibited any racial assignment in formerly desegregated schools that had been declared free of racial discrimination. This led to the move to drop race as a factor in school assignments in Wake County. Initially, the U.S. Department of Education's Office of Civil Rights challenged Wake's policy on the grounds that the new income-based criterion was simply a proxy for race and hence discriminated against whites by giving preferential treatment to blacks. However, on review, Wake was cleared of all discrimination charges, based on its defense of the clear relevance of socioeconomic status to academic achievement among all ethnic groups.[5]

Nonetheless, some critics, including a vocal minority in Raleigh, protested that school assignments based on economic diversity constituted unnecessary and intrusive "social engineering." They pointed to a few urban charter schools that have achieved good academic outcomes with a mostly black student body. These lighthouse schools could be found in nearly every city, but they gave false hope to children trapped in collapsing urban schools because they were very difficult to replicate. These charter schools often succeeded under unusually gifted principals who established requirements such as Saturday classes that drew children from only the most structured homes. Their parents may have been poor but they were highly motivated to take on the cost of transportation and other burdens in order to meet the special demands of charter schools. Meanwhile, the mass of poor children from less stable homes attended schools with beat-up lockers, lower expectations, and high proportions of unqualified teachers. McNeal grew up in a system of "have and have-not schools" in nearby Durham and came to believe that Wake's new policy could eliminate the latter. "And I would resign if Wake backed off that commitment," he said quietly.

In the jargon of sociology, the merged Wake County school system redistributed social capital by changing the networks of opportunity for poor and minority children. Merely pouring dollars into economically segregated urban schools could no more provide equal educational opportunity than spending dollars to maintain "separate but equal" racially segregated schools had done in the 1950s—although many urban schools need and deserve more dollars to help the children they have. Teachers in Wake came to believe that having a good mix of students in every school gave them the best chance of success in reaching the high goals that the countywide system had set for itself.

While McNeal agreed that balance was critical, he knew that neither a 95 percent goal nor a policy of economic diversity would create results without major changes in how schools operated. Chief among these was providing teachers with resources and giving them the freedom to create programs they were proud of while holding them accountable for results. In visits to a wide variety of schools in Wake County, I began to understand what he meant.

Inside Schools

Kids of all colors were pouring off the buses as I arrived at North Ridge Elementary School on Harps Mill Road in an upscale community a few miles north of the Beltline. The principal, Jane Slay, met me with a twinkle in her eye and gave me the tour. The lapels of her gray plaid jacket flapped in the wind as we walked in and out of classrooms whose doors opened onto the playground. Slightly more than half the 729 students enrolled were minority, she told me, and 36 percent were close enough to the poverty line to receive subsidized lunches. Last year when that number crept up to 43 percent, low-income enrollment had been reduced to bring the school back into balance with Wake County's poverty cap of 40 percent.

I asked about black students at North Ridge, whose passing rate on state exams had risen 21 points, almost closing the gap with their affluent white peers. How did you get there? She turned and took me down the sidewalk to a large room where students were filing in and logging onto computers. "This computer lab is our safety net. Children go in here three times a week for half an hour—15 minutes on math and 15 minutes on reading. The computer tracks them and figures out what level they're on. The kids get positive feedback on what they get right. And it pushes them to the next level. The teacher gets a printout of what skills kids are missing—it could be reading for detail, or failing to understand graphing."

"So it's basically testing, then?" I asked. "No, no, no," she replied, raising both hands as if to push me away. "It's basically diagnostic, finding out what a child needs to be successful in reading and math." Success came from sharing the data and putting the real problems on the table so that teachers could deal with them. "Teachers decide what programs and methods we're going to use. We do a lot of brainstorming. So when we identify a problem, I ask, 'How do we solve it?' Then you've got to have the nerve to do it."

Several years ago the North Ridge staff decided they had to provide benchmarks for each child to aim at. They began with children who were failing but were also concerned about pushing children who were just passing to higher levels. "So if I'm a teacher with 27 kids and 9 of them are below grade level, I'm going to be writing to and meeting with those parents about what is needed for their child to be successful and ready to move on next year. We explain what benchmarks your child needs to reach in reading, math and writing by October. And where they should be by December."

Slay went on to talk about ways parents had helped their children—by listening to them read or making sure they completed their assigned homework. Most were cooperative but "we had some parents who were belligerent. They had not had a good experience in school themselves and didn't think their child was having a good one. They may come in and get a little out of hand." She paused, took a deep breath: "Teachers here work hard to convince parents we're the best friends you have in educating your child. We don't rant and rave. We listen to what they have to say and then try to explain what has to happen for your child to be successful." It took a while to get there, Slay said, but teachers at North Ridge came to believe deeply that all children could reach a level of success. "This is what we ought to be doing. This is the way our children should be performing. And parents come to see we believe that, too."

I thought of my conversation with Slay a few days later when I visited Washington Elementary School, where Bob Bridges had taught in 1961 when it was still a segregated black inner-city school. It bordered the Walnut Terrace housing project, where 40 percent of the school's students lived. Most of the rest were bused in from the suburbs, and because of Washington's reputation as an outstanding magnet school, hundreds more were on the waiting list to get in the following year.

Paul Bartlett, a tall, blond fourth-grade teacher wearing a white shirt and patterned blue tie, put his suburban students on a bus and then walked the rest of his class across the street to make sure they got safely back to their homes in Walnut Terrace. As we climbed the stairs to his classroom, Bartlett told me that two of his own children were attending Washington. He sometimes took them along when he made home visits to the housing project, which he did nearly every week to keep parents informed about their child's progress. He had graduated from Tulane with honors in political science and had been teaching at Washington for eight years. When we reached Bartlett's classroom, five students were waiting for homework club to begin. The walls were lined with fish-print paintings and photographs of a recent class trip to Kitty Hawk. Remains of a physics experiment—rockets children constructed with Alka-Seltzer and cardboard tubes to see who could make the best launch of a small payload—lay on a table.

Some of the students were working on a problem from the last class before the bell. They had each been given two cookies to cut into thirds. "If I tell you to eat one third of your cookies, how many pieces do you eat?" LeVon had figured it out: "Two pieces." Bartlett pushed him: "How do two pieces, or two sixths, equal one third?" When LeVon showed how he reduced the fraction, Bartlett congratulated him for staying on task while he was putting kids on the bus and gave him a smiley sticker. "Three more of these and you get to go with us to play the laser game, LeVon." For the remainder of the hour, students were working on the next day's homework. That's why Bartlett started the club, which met four afternoons each week, to make sure that these children didn't fall behind. Laser games, bowling, and trips to the movies helped keep them coming. Bartlett asked me to help Zante with his reading. I found that he was stuck on words like "frazzled" and "relief."

Over the course of several visits, Bartlett became increasingly candid about the changes in belief and teaching practices he had undergone. When I offered to turn off the tape he said he was willing to continue but asked me not to use his real name. There were times he thought about quitting. The pay was not great and the burdens could be killing. "It's a constant struggle with kids from poverty. Some years you have kids from hell. I had a kid two years ago who made every day a living hell. I would just ask him to take out a piece of paper and he would explode, shouting, knocking things over, storms out of class. The reality is, he hasn't done his homework and he's scared, covering it with his anger."

Bartlett came to realize that "every teacher is hoping every year they will have the perfect class. You have this vision and then you have this kid who screws everything up. What I realized was you're never going to have that perfect class. Could be a white or black kid, high or low performing kid, but if you realize that's part of your challenge, it makes it a lot easier." It was also easier at a place like Washington, where less than a quarter of his children were below grade level—unlike in an urban school system where a majority of the students were below grade level and absenteeism rates were high. He was proud to be in a school with "great colleagues and parent support—everybody wants to be here."

Bartlett's reputation grew as his skills grew. He became a team leader and passed rigorous exams to earn National Board certification. Yet when he heard the School Board had set the goal of having 95 percent of all students pass state exams, he was skeptical. "I didn't think it was realistic. I thought we were doing everything we could for these kids." He worried that "everything is going to be seen through the goggle of state tests." All the data about every school in Wake County was published in the newspapers or was made available on the web. "They haven't got to the point of publishing each teacher's scores, but you hear how you're doing from the principal."

Bartlett had always received top evaluations as a teacher, and a new black vice principal who sat in on his classes not long after the 95 percent goal was adopted had been complimentary. "But before she left she told me, 'You are really doing a good job with the high achieving kids but how are you helping the low-achieving kids?' She may even have said the black kids. She thought I could do a better job and it really pissed me off. I thought I was knocking myself out. It stuck in my craw and then I thought about it and looked again at the scores of those kids and I realized I'm really not. I was writing them off." That's when he started the homework club.

He also began to tackle the job of targeting more classroom instruction toward those low-achieving students. "What's hard is differentiating instruction for different levels. You're really planning three different homework assignments and teaching three or even five different lessons." Bartlett said his strength had always been challenging the high-performing kids. He could "ask questions all day to push them to next level." He began to have lunch with the low-achievers to figure out how to reach them. He developed reading contracts and asked parents to sign them. He searched for resources that would help them. "It's a lot of extra work. It's not just giving the low-level kid extra homework problems but creating a whole different style of teaching and interacting."

Bartlett was not the only teacher making these changes. The school as a whole was becoming data-driven. "It was no longer just how many passed but breaking data down into gender, ethnicity, and race, looking at particular pieces of the curriculum so you could see these third grade black boys are struggling with decimals or whatever. That was a huge change." Yet there was time for fish-scale prints and rockets, too. It was not all about the tests: "We're teaching in a way that's more aligned with the tests but we're teaching a good curriculum, not just teaching for the test."

Teaching at Washington had become less isolating once the goals were adopted, Bartlett felt. There was a lot more sharing about why some teachers had spectacular success as well as pinpointing reasons for failures. A staff support team met often to discuss children who were having problems and to figure out ways to help. The system was changing to put more resources behind these students. At Washington, half the school day was given to electives. All children took three electives in the afternoon. Low-performing children could choose one elective in art or dance or geography, but if they were behind in either reading or math, they had to choose an elective in these areas, thus doubling the instruction time they most needed. The Boys and Girls Club was encouraged to set up trailers on the school grounds where Washington children could play games but also get tutoring after school and on Saturdays. Thirty or forty parent volunteers came into the school each week. Bartlett's principal set aside some of her budget to hire additional teachers in January to handle the continual in-migration of new students and provide extra remedial help to those who were still behind. At Washington and other Wake schools, low-achieving students received as much as 25 percent more resources to get them to grade level before they left elementary school.

Long-term evaluations of early interventions, such as a forty-year study of the effects of the Perry Preschool in Ypsilanti, Michigan, have shown dramatic benefits. Compared with a matched sample, those who benefited from the high-quality Perry program were half as likely to go to jail as adults and earned an average of 27 percent more than the nonattenders. I predict that Raleigh will need to build fewer prisons in the future than Syracuse.

Can the High Schools Do It Too?

Wake County's unprecedented achievement in its elementary and middle schools was widely celebrated. Some skeptics who offered their congratulations admitted they never thought the schools would get there. The School Board took a deep breath and then set a similar five-year goal for its high schools. By 2008, 95 percent of all high school students would pass state end-of-course exams in all major subjects.

Anyone who has studied school reform knows that it is harder to change high schools. While pay differentials between elementary and high school teachers have been erased in most public school systems, high school teachers still enjoy more status and autonomy as experts in their subject areas. High schools sort students into different tracks or ability levels, and the best teachers—or sometimes just those with the most seniority—carve out careers teaching only upper-level honors or Advanced Placement students. They can (and do) frustrate reform-minded principals. But even if high schools teachers in Wake County had wanted to do so, there was no way for them to turn back the tide of reform. They could not refuse to try to do what their colleagues in the elementary and middle schools had achieved. They could no longer rely on the excuse that teachers in the grade schools had not done their job or claim that incoming students were not prepared for high school.

I saw little resistance to reform in the five high schools I visited. On the contrary, they had begun to adapt the kinds of approaches that had worked in the grade schools. This was nowhere more evident than at Broughton High, once a segregated high school for the white elite in an old west Raleigh neighborhood. It is still an outstanding high school with a wide range of Advanced Placement courses and the intellectually challenging International Baccalaureate program. While a third of Broughton students are nonwhite and nearly a fifth are from poor families, the white elite has not abandoned the school.[6]

Some students sat eating lunch on the edge of brick planters, others at picnic tables in the sunny Broughton courtyard when I stopped to ask the way to Loren Baron's history class. By the time I got to the third floor, his class was already under way. Baron looked to be in his late thirties, athletic with some gray in short-cropped hair. He stood in the middle of the classroom, next to a laptop, bouncing on the balls of his feet, hands in his pockets, wearing a tie and brown jogging shoes, telling the students they needed to know the quirky details and personalities of those who made the decisions that shaped history. The walls were covered with posters of Brazil, Colombia, Myanmar, and South Korea. Baron traveled widely after finishing a degree in history and philosophy at Brandeis University. He learned Chinese and taught for a year in China, traveled throughout India, and worked in Australia. He told his students that the best way to go abroad is to get a job if you can, or at least use only the local buses to break out of the tourist world in whatever countries you visit.

Baron easily handled the laptop, flashing pictures of Czar Nicholas, Emperor Franz Josef, and Kaiser Wilhelm and maps of Austria and Hungary on the wall as he talked about the origins of the First World War. He paused over a photograph of the Archduke Franz Ferdinand, the nephew of Franz Josef, in a large touring car with Sophie, an outcast in the royal family whose children could not succeed to the throne. He told the story of how they had taken the wrong street and while cumbersomely trying to turn around in an alley, a man walked out of a coffee-shop and shot the archduke point blank. The students were gripped, engaged.

When we sat down to talk later, I complimented him on a terrific class. He told a complex story well, cutting away to reveal fascinating subplots while keeping the big picture in focus. Baron thanked me politely then smiled wryly. The new emphasis on tests had put more pressure on coverage: "I have had to speed up a bit. I can't spend as much time on World War I yet at the same time there's stuff I can't not teach. So I tell the kids this may sacrifice three points on the E.O.C. [End of Course state exam] but I'm going to teach it anyway." He feared that some teachers were teaching too superficially in order to cover 100 percent of the curriculum outline. "I tend to be one of those who want to cover 50 percent extremely well." He was no fan of the multiple-choice state tests, which put too much emphasis on facts and not enough on reasoning or essay writing, which would be more costly to grade. Yet he recognized they were necessary and had forced a major redistribution of teaching resources to better serve low-performing students.

116

Senior teachers in the history department, as in most of the academic departments at Broughton, no longer had the privilege of teaching only honors or advanced classes. All taught a mix of classes, and all taught some low-performing students in "on-level" or general track classes. Teachers were jointly planning classes and developing unit tests together for the first time. "So we are very cognizant of the tests but at the same time very uncomfortable with the idea of just teaching to the test." Yet Baron recognized that the new test requirements were changing the teaching culture at Broughton and making all teachers more accountable. It was not just about passing the test but pushing all students to a higher level of achievement.

How had this affected his teaching? He had become a history teacher because he loved history. He used to spend every spare moment reading more history, learning more. But Baron told me that he now spent more time thinking about "teaching strategies that are going to work for these lower level kids." Baron asked himself whether he was "teaching in a way that kids will remember this two months from now." He was trying to be more concrete, use films and photographs, and get kids to think like historians. In a United States history class I watched him put up a picture of the meeting of the Union Pacific and Central Pacific railroads at Promontory Point, Utah, in 1869. He asked, "What do you see? Raise your hand." Long silence. Baron started waving his arm like a kid wanting to speak. The students laughed. Baron called on himself to answer. "I see a train." More laughter. "OK, what do you see?" A girl said, "I see white people," and described what they were wearing and what that might indicate about their status. A boy near her guessed what time of day it was by the shadows the shrubs cast.

Baron had learned to ask questions in a way that "works lower level students into it." He told them they were going to be wrong sometimes. "Everyone is wrong sometimes. I'm not going to su-garcoat that." He waited longer for answers; he pushed harder. "If they don't answer the question the first time, I don't accept 'I don't know.' I may have to ask the question differently. But I'll keep asking the same students. I'll sit there for 30 seconds of si-lence and just wait." Whereas he once felt class time was too precious to spend on homework, he came to realize that some students were much more likely to complete homework assign-ments if they started work on them in class where he could help slower pupils get over a rough spot or just get past their initial doubt.

No sentimental egalitarian who believed in a random mix of all students, Baron recognized the wide gap between the poor students—many of them black or Latino—and the rich preppy whites at Broughton. Some of those poor students were do-ing well in honors and AP classes. But Baron felt that those who were below grade level needed the kind of special atten-tion, more wait time to answer questions, and in-class home-work help that might embarrass them in more randomly mixed classes. He again underscored how important it was to get all students to higher levels and to direct more resources and more efforts to those most likely to give up and drop out. "It isn't just a matter of you teach it and they take the test. You are probing in a variety of ways every day to see if they've learned it, and if they haven't, figure out ways to help them get it." A lot more of that kind of "figuring it out" was now going on in conversations with his colleagues. Teachers at Broughton High shared more.

While I knew that Baron was a gifted teacher, what I saw in his classroom could also be found in Broughton's science, math, and English classes. And not only at Broughton but at four other high schools I visited. Most were making significant changes in how they taught in order to reach the new goals. Baron was proud of his colleagues' accomplishments and wanted his own children to attend Broughton. "We are trying new strategies and we debate them and get angry sometimes if they don't work. We may get tired but there's a lot of energy here. I don't know if we'll make the goal [95 percent passing state exams] but we will keep trying." Nearly 94 percent of all tenth graders at Broughton passed the state math test in 2006, but only 83 percent of black students and 77 percent of students in poverty. However, the results in English Language Arts were not as impressive: just 76 percent of the class passed, and only 51 percent of blacks and 45 percent of poor students. Overall, 82 percent of high school students were on grade level in English in 2006.

Baron had taught for ten years in the Washington suburb of Montgomery County before coming to the Wake school district. Montgomery was a good school system but flawed by "rigid gate-keeping." He found it less responsive and more bureaucratic than Wake. When he decided to leave, he searched the web for high schools in Wake with International Baccalaureate programs. He sent emails to the principals of Broughton and Enloe high schools on a Wednesday, and by the following Monday he was interviewing at both schools. On Tuesday the Broughton principal made him a job offer. While focused on the new goal, the school remained flexible about offering teachers opportunities to teach new electives. It took him only a few months to develop an elective on the Civil War. "I can talk to people here. The central office support staff is accessible. I never had that flexibility in Montgomery County. It was just very cumbersome." In his old school, he didn't feel known. When he earned National Board certification as a highly accomplished teacher at Montgomery, he got five letters of congratulation from administrators, all of them addressed to "Ms. Baron."

More importantly, Baron saw Wake as a system that not only

redirected resources to the neediest children but also provided funds and opportunities for teacher development. Wake did more to attract and develop effective teachers.

How Did Wake County Make It Happen?

School reforms usually fall into one of three types: fix a broken system, disrupt the system, or replace the system. Raleigh did all three. It replaced two systems leaning toward failure with a completely new merged system. It disrupted the old ways of doing business by introducing competition, giving parents a choice by turning a third of its schools into magnet schools. And it fixed the system with new forms of teaching and management.[7]

The primary cause of Raleigh's success was having the courage and political will to merge city and suburban schools in 1976. That step alone probably accounted for more than half the test score gains. It enabled Wake to create the right balance of racial, ethnic, and economic assets in every school, so that no one school was overwhelmed by the neediest students. Social capital was redistributed fairly throughout city and county in a way that almost no urban school system outside the South had achieved. Social capital is the yeast that makes a good school rise.

The belief that "there are no bad public schools in Wake County" was widely held by parents and teachers. In urban systems where bad schools are easily identified—by low test scores, high dropout rates, concentrations of children in poverty, more crime and violence—good teachers often leave for job offers in the suburbs. As a result of this talent flight, schools serving the neediest children in the urban core are disproportionately staffed with teachers who are least qualified or poorly prepared to teach the subjects they have been assigned to teach.[8] In Raleigh, where parents put their children on waiting lists to attend inner-city schools, no teachers felt that they were in a "losing school" where the deck was stacked against them because the school had been virtually abandoned by middle-class families. Nor did they hesitate to bring their own children to school with them. Teacher absenteeism was a small fraction of what it was in Syracuse, where teachers called in sick frequently, remarking to colleagues that they needed a "mental health day."

The second important step that Wake County took was to create magnet schools offering choice among distinctive educational options. In Raleigh, it was not just token choice. Magnets had failed to achieve major desegregation in many other cities because there were only a few of them, often located in the inner city. Raleigh created a critical mass of magnet schools, particularly in the early years of merger, by turning nearly a third of the schools into schools of choice. The top leadership spent a year selling the wide variety of choices to black and white parents, convincing them that these were opportunities they couldn't afford to turn down.

All the magnets were opened in the following year and were placed in schools along the border between the city and suburbs. Neither city nor suburban children had to be bused far. The principle of two-way busing, with white children being bused into the city while black children rode to schools in the suburbs, was enshrined in Raleigh's program from the beginning. The magnet program was not just a device to achieve racial balance, however. Magnet schools became laboratories to test new programs and new approaches to teaching. Programs that succeeded were exported to other schools in the system, and those that failed were later jettisoned.

Often overlooked was the opportunity for choice that the magnets offered teachers as well as parents and students. The magnet programs helped Wake recruit able teachers like Loren Baron who were looking for the right niche, and gave other teachers within the system the chance to grow in new directions. In later years, magnets helped reduce the tension that afflicted some districts about the impositions of testing. Even children who were getting double the instruction in math and reading in order to catch up also got to choose a dance class or a course in filmmaking. And teachers were given plentiful opportunities to create such courses.

Third, instead of complaining about statewide testing, Wake County used it to set a gutsy goal and mobilize the community at a time when many doubted that 95 percent of its children could pass the state tests. This occurred four years before the No Child Left Behind federal law was passed. Studies of failed reforms have revealed that they were often poorly introduced without negotiating the prior agreements that lead teachers to buy in. Raleigh created the Wake Partnership uniting the business sector, political leadership, parents, and teachers. Thousands came to public meetings to discuss the new goal. It helped the whole community to own it, by convincing them that the schools could not do it alone. Teachers told me in interviews how galvanizing these meetings were. This wasn't a pet project of a new principal or a phony experiment in a few schools that administrators knew were close to achieving the goal already. It applied to everyone, to all schools. Teachers accepted that it made sense to break the goal into two five-year periods, getting the elementary and middle schools up to speed by 2003 and the high schools by 2008. Everyone agreed that the best way to reform high schools is to reform grade schools first. It was a stunningly clear and simple goal that allowed schools to choose different means to achieving it.[9]

Likewise, all were being held accountable—not only teachers

but also principals and the top leadership. Even Superintendent McNeal agreed to have his salary pegged to the achievement levels of all students. For years, McNeal had led the system toward a more data-driven curriculum. Wake had one of the most advanced databases of any school system in the nation. Its website—far ahead of what most school systems had at that time—provided detailed profiles of each school with in-depth analyses of its test scores and with comments posted by students and parents about safety and teachers' attitudes.

Important as data were, however, Wake did not see success on the new tests as the goal of reform but as a *means* to reform. Real reform went deeper. It involved a change from older models of management toward new cultures of leadership and teaching. Change in management styles began before the new goal was announced. Principals were taught how to use their computers to analyze the new data in ways that would improve instruction. Control of the budget was decentralized as Wake moved to school site management—that is, principals were given authority to make major shifts in their budgets to put more resources at the service of low-achieving pupils. They took advantage of seminars conducted at the central office to learn new skills.

The school district created the Wake Leadership Academy, a new training program for aspiring principals using its own cutting-edge staff and faculty at North Carolina State University. These principals-in-training went out in teams to analyze top-performing schools as well as failing ones in Raleigh and other school districts. They learned how to conduct the kind of collaborative inquiry that helped teachers develop. While classroom visits and one-on-one supervision of teachers, particularly new hires, continued to be an important part of a principal's work, Raleigh principals increasingly became managers and nurturers of teaching teams, each of which had its own teacher-leader or co-leaders. The team might be composed entirely of fourth grade teachers, or of cross-grade teams of elementary math instructors, or of high school biology teachers.

The teams were at the heart of the change in the teaching culture of Wake County. For generations teachers had worked in a system that sorted and selected students, while for the most part ignoring the dropout rate. Even the word "dropout" didn't come into widespread use until the 1960s. Up until that time, half or more of all students were expected to fail or drop out, and when they did it was the pupil's fault for not learning what teachers taught. Not much was known about what teachers were actually teaching, or how they were going about it. They worked in isolation, and only rarely engaged in joint planning or evaluation with colleagues. Experienced teachers seldom shared their practical wisdom or special techniques with novices. Only in recent decades has teaching all students to succeed become a goal. In many places it is still an empty mantra.

Wake County's adoption of the 95 percent goal in 1998 put the nail in the coffin of the old teacher belief system in Raleigh. Making it work was another thing altogether, however. Part of the task was to align what was taught with what got tested, and some teachers felt the screws were tightened too much. But most Raleigh teachers I interviewed felt that they were teaching a good curriculum and that the tests were fair. Getting most kids to pass those tests, however, was a stretch for many teachers.[10] Even prior to 1998 some Wake schools with more than a third of their students from low-income and minority families had come close to the 95 percent goal. Teachers were encouraged to visit those schools. Many found it a transforming experience—seeing is believing. Some had the courage to tell their colleagues that they had seen teachers who were doing what those colleagues were doing—only better. The creation of teacher teams moved that kind of realistic assessment to the core of conversations.

Several years after I first visited Paul Bartlett's classroom at Washington Elementary I heard that he had been selected for the Wake Leadership Academy and was now an assistant principal deeply involved in trying to create effective teacher teams. He opened my eyes to the dimensions of that challenge and the resistance many teachers had to such a radical change in their practice. It wasn't just a lack of trust that prevented teachers from comparing what they were doing and the results they were getting. Changing their practice often meant giving up a closet full of lesson plans that individual teachers had developed over the years and felt comfortable with. "It's tough to ask teachers to put away a career's worth of materials and create new stuff." Bartlett said he was one of those teachers: "I was an effective teacher doing it my way with lessons I loved. The kids liked me and the parents were more than happy. I could have gone on doing my curriculum on autopilot. So why should I change?"

A large part of the motivation came from buying into the dream, coming to believe that a 95 percent pass rate wasn't just pie-in-the-sky, that they were actually accomplishing something that urban public schools had never done before: educating all the kids. Motivation also came from the satisfaction of being part of a community of teachers who are sharing knowledge and learning together. It was not just "Implement this new program and shut up." It was about sitting down together with data print-outs in hand, analyzing weaknesses, thinking about the kids, sharing best practices, coming up with ideas of what might work better, trying some of them, and seeing what works.

When he was a lone teacher in the classroom, Bartlett was always hoping to get back to the kids who weren't making it, but he almost never did. The team wouldn't let a teacher forget. "We look at the data and see that 80 percent have gotten a certain concept. Then we ask what kind of further instruction should we do for the other 20 percent." He acknowledged that tough team oversight may have driven out some creative teachers. "But we are also developing new talent and new teacher leaders who think about effective teaching in new ways. And long-term you have to ask what kind of system do you want. If your goal is to impact all kids and reach a high level of performance, you need definable and measurable goals. Creativity comes in how you reflect on that data. To achieve what Wake County has achieved a teacher has to make that shift." He added that it was critical for the system to provide more resources to help teachers get there.

Administrators at the top of the Wake County system were bold in moving major resources to help teachers, in some cases increasing a school's budget by as much as 25 percent in one year. Those resources enabled schools to double the instructional time in math and reading for low-performing children. Some children were placed in year-round schools to help them catch up. This often required persuading parents that giving up a long vacation period now would pay off later. And Wake backed up teachers and principals who asked parents to sign "contracts" to help ensure that children watched less television and did more homework.[11] The leadership of the system also achieved success in drawing an usually large proportion of parents of all income levels to schools as volunteers. They carved out meaningful roles for those parents, who in turn became enthusiastic supporters of what Wake was trying to do for all children.

Parents of high-achieving children saw that closing the basic proficiency gap (that's what state tests measure—it doesn't mean all children take calculus) was neither choking imaginative teaching nor putting a cap on achievement. Children moved far beyond basic proficiency in math and reading to Advanced Placement courses and challenging programs in magnet schools. A higher proportion of children from affluent families were in those advanced courses but the numbers of poor and black and Latino children enrolling in them increased. Parents of many low-scoring children saw that teachers taught their children more effectively than they themselves had been taught a generation ago. They saw that tests were being used to improve instruction in major ways and not to penalize students. The goal was to not pass them by or push them out.

Did students see it that way? In order to learn their views, I briefly taught a junior year English class at Broughton. It was an on-level class in which more than two thirds of the students were black and Latino. I asked them to write a letter to a cousin who was moving to Raleigh. "I'm worried about whether I'll fit in and how kids and teachers will treat me," the cousin asked. "Give me the skinny on Broughton and what it feels like to be a student there." I offered Barnes and Noble gift certificates as prizes for the best essays.

The students took up the challenge with gusto, pounding away on laptops in the school library. They described a school with black folks, punks, smokers, druggies, and rich white preps who arrived at Broughton in their "BMWs and Hummers wearing their Polo's and Sperry's and Rainbows." The lunchroom was "like being in a 96-count box of Crayola Crayons." There was a fair amount of interracial dating but also occasional racial incidents and some "abusive language." Nearly all of them liked Broughton and wouldn't leave even if offered a scholarship to a leading private school. Broughton was very safe, yet "Don't get me wrong. People are going to have fights. But they're usually pity pats."

They didn't say much about tests, but the message about caring, responsive teachers who wanted them to succeed came through in many essays. A black girl who said she was "not one of the wealthiest" students at Broughton, and who was both aggressive and something of a clown in class, wrote: "I think in my three years here I've had the best teachers that a school could offer. They take the time to get to know you. Especially Ms. Matkins. She passed away last year. She was one of the funniest, goofiest persons I had ever met in my life. How many teachers do you know that tell you to call them on the weekends and in the summer. She would take me to conventions at the district and state level." But it wasn't just Ms. Matkins: "There is always someone around that is willing to help you with your studies. That is what I love about my school. All the teachers expect is that all of their students do well and not just one race. No matter what your financial status is, you are not going to be treated differently."

Her comments were echoed in other essays, including one written by a quiet boy whose red hair fell in long strands over his eyes. He dated a girl "whose mom is white and dad is black and as far as I know nobody criticizes me for it." He wore a striped blue T-shirt from K-Mart and objected to the pressure some felt to dress like preps. But he had high praise for his teachers: "I don't have one teacher that doesn't care about my grades. If you need to come in after school and get help or tutoring from them they are usually willing to. The same expectations are given to everyone. All of my teachers don't treat any of us differently because we are a different race or rich or poor. I have heard of some teachers that have treated kids differently for being a different race but I think this is very rare. Teachers look at your effort not your skin."

Superintendent McNeal was far from complacent about Wake's achievements. In our last interview before his retirement, he confessed: "It could all come unglued." He pointed to resegregation occurring in Charlotte, where a School Board member suggested "mothballing" some of the inner-city schools that had emptied out. "That could happen again here," he said. McNeal also worried about the recent uptick in private school enrollment in Wake. He was even more concerned about the heavy coverage that Cynthia Matson was getting in local media for her attacks on the pupil assignment policies that kept Wake's schools in racial and economic balance. Matson was the head of Assignment By Choice, an organization she created to challenge current school policy. McNeal had read her website and knew that it got a lot of hits.

Matson, a mother of two young children, moved to Raleigh in 1989 from the Boston suburb of Lexington to start an electrical contracting business with her husband. Twenty-four members of her extended family followed, including her father, a polymer chemist. Her mother was chairperson of Assignment By Choice, a title chosen to emphasize Matson's belief that children were getting "assigned" to schools in the Wake system without their parents having any real choice.

Matson was blunt when we met at a crowded restaurant in suburban Cary. "They say we have choices but we do not. They control the choice, and they're forcing people against their will, against their wishes, putting kids on buses for up to two hours each way." She believed McNeal and his "social engineering" had to go. Her organization had helped elect two School Board members friendly to her cause, and she hoped to oust the rest of them in the next election. I asked her about critics who said she was just another Yankee who had bought an expensive house in Cary and expected it to come with a mostly white, up-scale school, as did homes in Boston's exclusive suburbs. She replied that she has a nice house but it didn't cost that much, and her son attended Swift Creek Elementary, a school with high minority enrollment. "I am so sick of these people saying I'm doing this because I'm a racist or because I don't want my kid brought down by kids who are struggling."

Her campaign started at home after her son got rejected several times to schools she had hoped would help him with his attention deficit and hearing problems. She applied to Washington Elementary, which had too many children on the waiting list, and to Oak Grove, a year-round school. When she applied a second time to Oak Grove, as her son was entering first grade, the enrollment of white children was severely restricted, she believed, to achieve more balance of low-income and black children. A significant degree of diversity could be achieved through choice, she said, but "what we have now is more like socialism."

Superintendent McNeal was quick to acknowledge that not every parent was satisfied and that some, like Matson, suffered some hardship. Partly as a result of Matson's criticism, Wake opened up its pupil-assignment process, holding more public hearings and giving parents more opportunity to appeal a grievance. "Thousands of parents are coming to Wake every year, and they insist on bringing their children with them," McNeal said with just a hint of a smile. "We have to find a place for them, and that requires us to make reassignments as we open new schools." Most parents get their choice: 80 percent of Wake's students attend a neighborhood school, which may also be a magnet school. Another 15 percent voluntarily apply for and transfer into other magnet programs outside their neighborhoods. Only 5 percent are assigned solely to achieve socioeconomic balance. Surveys of parents show that most are highly satisfied with their child's school, including those who did not get one of their top choices.

Because of a bumper crop of new students and heavy media coverage, Matson's supporters hoped a thousand or more might turn out for the pupil reassignment hearings in 2004. But less than 200 showed up, some to thank the School Board for granting their appeals. Only a few black parents protested, citing a lengthy bus ride for children assigned to a year-round school. Matson's supporters, echoing her complaints about social engineering, came armed with data and maps to claim that busing reduced parent voluntarism and increased traffic hazards. It was not the rousing turnout that Matson wanted, but she continued to press her campaign to elect a new School Board and threatened to bring suit against a policy of busing to achieve socioeconomic balance.

She got under the skin of more than a few Raleigh educators, who expressed the wish that Matson and her followers would go back where they came from. Yet most also understood that conflict was inevitable in a democracy. As the political theorist Albert O. Hirschman wrote, those with grievances have two choices: voice or exit. You can seek change by using your voice in the democratic forum, or you can exit for what you see as greener pastures. There continues to be a vigorous exercise of voice in Raleigh. In Syracuse, most have chosen exit.

Matson's organization drew new recruits in the fall of 2006 when McNeal's successor, Del Burns, proposed a billion dollar bond issue to build new schools to keep up with Wake's rapid population growth. Opposition to the bond issue was fueled by two factors: resentment over the need to reassign more pupils to maintain economic balance, and a cost-saving proposal—linked to the bond issue—that would convert all elementary schools to year-round operation. An elementary school with a capacity of 900 students could serve 1,200 if it operated year-round, with a fourth of the students on break at different times throughout the year. When Wake County had only a few year-round schools, it had no problem filling them up with children whose parents liked the idea of shorter breaks. But year-round schools that required many students to be on long leaves during the fall, winter, or spring were another matter.

A new protest group, Stop Mandatory Year-Round, quickly gained a large following. When a Raleigh *News and Observer* poll showed that the bond issue was likely to be defeated, Burns got the message and sharply reduced the number of schools that would operate on a year-round basis.[12] Meanwhile, supporters of the bond issue countered with arguments that Raleigh's continued prosperity was closely tied to its maintenance of a top-quality school system that avoided resegregation. The billion dollar bond issue passed comfortably with 53 percent approval that November. The highest support, over 60 percent in favor, came from voters inside the Beltline.[13]

Matson's organization was rebuffed in both the bond vote and School Board elections. Two of the three new board members favored strong diversity and income-balance guidelines. However, maintaining that balance was becoming more difficult. Wake County was enjoying one of the highest growth rates in the nation. It had 57,000 students in 1985 and more than 130,000 by 2008; the number was projected to rise to 250,000 by 2025. The county was attracting families not only from the Northeast and Midwest but increasingly from Mexico and Central America. The percentage of low-income children rose to 27 percent in 2007. The number of schools with more than 40 percent of students qualifying for subsidized school lunches doubled in six years. Fifteen of Wake's 136 schools exceeded the low-income guideline in 2000. Thirty-one had crossed that threshold by 2006.[14] And there were other worrisome signs. In 2007 the percentage of all students passing end-of-course tests in grades 9–12 at Broughton High dropped to 75 percent. Only Green Hope High School had 90 percent passing. Four Wake high schools had overall passing rates of 80 to 90 percent, nine had 70 to 80 percent, three had 60 to 70 percent, and three had only 50 to 60 percent passing.[15] Looking back, McNeal said the failure to secure additional funding needed to reach the high school goal was the "critical mistake . . . we overreached."[16]

The Raleigh *News and Observer* has run major articles saying "Wake Schools Find Diversity Hard to Sustain" and asking "Is Diversity Worth the Effort?"[17] The bond vote affirmed that most still thought it was. In the debate, however, some urged that Wake be divided into several smaller school systems. If and how that is done could have major effects on the county's ability to maintain the kind of healthy balance it has achieved. Will city boosters still be able to say in 2025 that there are no bad schools in Raleigh?

5 A Tragic Decision

.

The story of the decline and fall of Syracuse is a tale of despair that afflicted much of urban America—especially cities in the Northeast and Midwest. These powerhouses of the industrial revolution changed the face of America in the nineteenth century, as workers left farms and immigrants came from abroad to seek higher paying jobs in the new factories. Industrial cities were the objects of a second great migration during and after World War II, when millions of blacks came north seeking those same jobs—now opened to them by federal laws that barred racial discrimination in defense plants or in any firm that received federal contracts.

The reasons why cities like Syracuse imploded are complex. They were hobbled by state laws that prohibited annexation or made it difficult, greatly reducing the tax base as new plants were built in suburbs where land was cheaper and taxes lower. They were swamped with brownfields saturated with chemical wastes from old industries. In Syracuse, the Solvay Process company, for example, left small mountains of pollutants on the shores of Onondaga Lake from its soda ash production. The urban infrastructure of dense older cities—from sewage pipes to roads and bridges—started to crumble and was costly to repair or replace. Cities failed to attract new industries and to make a transition to a more information-based economy. From 1970 to 2000 the Syracuse metropolitan area lost 30 percent of its manufacturing jobs, while Raleigh's industrial based grew by 93 percent. Northern and midwestern cities suffered from political corruption, bloated bureaucracies, and a failure of vision. In the last quarter of the twentieth century, the suburban middle class pictured cities as having a deserted downtown, abandoned houses, drug traffic, drive-by shootings, and concentrations of poor and minority children in bad schools. All of those things were true of Syracuse.

Nevertheless, the notion of middle-class flight has been overstated. Most people living in suburbs today were born there, although their parents or grandparents may have fled the city. Some left out of fear or racism: polls taken in the 1960s and 1970s showed that many whites did not want to live near blacks. The most common reasons cited were a drop in property values and an increase in crime.[1] Yet most of the people who held these views were not conscious racists, any more than I was when I bought a house in Skaneateles in 1972. They saw themselves as playing their part in the American dream: moving up to a higher standard of living, providing a safer environment for their children, and owning a half-acre of bliss. And—no small matter —they sought to enroll their children in newly minted public schools where parents would have a voice, which was not the case in an urban bureaucracy.

Perhaps these upwardly mobile migrants did not perceive or understand the long-term consequences when cities like Syracuse were unable to enrich their tax base and reduce concentrations of the poor by annexing suburban school districts. Not all suburbanites were aware of racist redlining practices that kept blacks from getting mortgages in the city, owning their own homes, and taking pride in the maintenance of their urban neighborhoods. Some may not have known the degree to which suburban zoning policies prevented poor and black people from buying affordable homes in affluent communities. Or how difficult it was for a poor or minority person to use a federally subsidized housing voucher to rent a home in the suburbs. Or the horrendous effects of destroying neighborhoods in the name of urban renewal, only to concentrate poor minorities in huge, barren housing projects overrun by gangs.

The result of these policies was to create an invisible wall between cities and suburbs. On one side of the wall were greater and greater concentrations of the poor and minorities—those with the greatest needs and a smaller tax base to provide resources. By the year 2000, more than half the children in Syracuse public schools were poor and minority, and three quarters of all fourth and eighth grade students failed state tests in reading and mathematics. On the other side of the wall, in the suburbs, where less than 2 percent were black and only 4 percent lived in poverty, 70 to 85 percent of schoolchildren passed the same tests. In Raleigh's schools—where city and suburban children were merged in a single countywide school system—more than 90 percent of students in grades 3 through 8 passed statewide exams by 2003. In the 1990s as New York and other states began to publish the scores for all their schools—with whole sections of newspapers devoted to detailing the results—not only suburban parents but more and more of those in the city concluded they would be bad parents if they did not make every effort to keep their children out of city schools.

Prescriptions for Urban Ills

Syracuse is a textbook example of misbegotten efforts to save America's cities through urban renewal in the 1960s. In retrospect, these federally funded programs look more like a transportation plan than anything that could be called renewal. Neighborhoods of the poor were bulldozed to provide more parking spaces for suburban commuters. Interstate highways made it easier for them to get to their offices by day, or to the symphony in the evening, and back home again without having to rub elbows with the city's poorest citizens. Later, as offices moved from cities to shinier accommodations in the suburbs, even the parking lots became empty eyesores.

In a new effort to revitalize the city beginning in the late 1990s, many reports were written and many experts spoke. Andres Duany came to present a plan based on the "New Urbanism." A team of architects spent a week assessing Syracuse and talking with local leaders about remedies. An "Under 40" group was formed to hear what would keep young talent from abandoning the city. Syracuse leaders joined together to form "20/20" whose aim was to develop a vision for the future. On one occasion the city convention center opened a kind of bazaar featuring various kinds of urban improvements. As citizens came through the door they were given tokens and invited to vote on their favorite reform by dropping the tokens into receptacles displayed at each booth. Apparently the Syracuse cyclists were well organized. The biggest vote by far was for more bike paths.

Major effort was expended on economic development. By 2006 New York's Empire Zone program provided tax breaks totaling more than $500 million annually to aid businesses to expand or relocate in high-poverty areas. But the program was flawed and produced few new jobs. One investigation showed that many businesses in the Syracuse area and elsewhere simply reincorporated under a slightly different name in a newly declared Empire Zone, claiming to start with zero employees, then "adding" those already hired at the old firm along with some new hires—what critics called "a change of shirt" that actually

137

did little to revitalize the community.[2] Syracuse gave tax breaks to the developers of Destiny USA who promised in the early 1990s to build not only a mall but a Disney-size development on the shores of Onondaga Lake that would be filled with office buildings, hotels, upscale restaurants, an aquarium, and a new harbor with 144 boat slips that would draw 35 million visitors a year. Fifteen years later it was still just a shopping mall.[3]

A Miami investor, Eli Hadad, created great excitement by purchasing sixteen historic buildings downtown, which he planned to turn into high-end apartments and condominiums, or so he said. A few years later nothing had been done, and he sold them all. Some empty-nesters had begun to return to the city but on nothing like the scale Hadad imagined. The distinguished 600-room Hotel Syracuse closed in 2004. A downtown arts corridor, announced with great fanfare, faltered when financing fell through. The biggest downtown employer, Excellus Blue Cross, moved to the suburbs. The assessed value of Syracuse's downtown properties fell by half, from $1.5 billion in 1976 to $729 million in 2007. This devaluation meant a loss of $28 million a year in tax revenues that could have helped rebuild Syracuse's schools and parks.[4]

In 2006, nearly fifty years after Raleigh established its Research Triangle Park linking North Carolina State to Duke University in Durham and the University of North Carolina at Chapel Hill, Syracuse announced its own triangle linking Syracuse University with the University of Rochester and Cornell University. However, this initiative focused on the humanities, not on the kinds of scientific research and technological innovation that drew new firms to Raleigh. While a new humanities center was a worthwhile enterprise, it did not do much for economic development.[5] A few new firms came to Syracuse, but the area continued to lose some of its biggest employers, and in the case of

Carrier Air Conditioning Syracuse's loss was North Carolina's gain. Bristol Meyers Squibb pharmaceutical company kept some of its Syracuse operation in business but chose to build a new $660 million plant for 550 workers in Massachusetts. Nestle Chocolate closed the doors on 467 employees. Nearly 300 people lost jobs when Syracuse China, one of the city's oldest firms, shut down in 2008.

Some developments, such as a new convention facility named Oncenter, were built and took off. What had been largely a warehouse district in downtown Syracuse was developed into a lively arts and entertainment district called Armory Square. Clinton Square in the heart of the city underwent a major redesign, with water fountains programmed to create different patterns of spray similar to those in New York's Lincoln Center. It became a place where people wanted to gather and where music festivals drew large crowds. A decades-long effort to clean up Onondaga Lake started to show results as fish returned to what had been one of the most polluted lakes in the nation. Syracuse University established a new bus route called the Connective Corridor that made it easier for the university's 15,000 students to connect with downtown.

Decline was reversed in Westcott and a few other neighborhoods in Syracuse. As citizens pushed the city to improve code enforcement, streets were repaved and crumbling sidewalks restored. Low-cost loans and grants, both state and federal, helped low-income homeowners to paint their houses, repair sagging porches, replace leaky roofs, and fix broken plumbing. Some new housing went up on cleared lots in the city. But these neighborhood improvements were marginal. The city as whole was still depressed. More than a thousand houses in the inner city were vacant and boarded up, and the landscape throughout the city was pockmarked with vacant lots. There was no significant return of young homesteaders or the middle class to Syracuse. Its overall population continued to decline in the early years of the twenty-first century, with the sharpest drop among those aged 18–24. Nearly half of Syracuse's ninth graders failed to graduate from high school.

The economic health of the city was among the worst in the nation. A 2007 study by the Brookings Institution ranked all cities in the United States on two indicators of economic success. The first measured growth in employment and in annual payroll. The second measured economic well-being based on median family income, the depth of poverty in each city, and unemployment. Of the 302 cities with more than 50,000 residents, Syracuse ranked 297th on growth and 279th on well-being. Raleigh ranked 13th on growth and 24th on well-being.[6]

Why Revitalization Efforts Failed

Like most of the distressed cities on the bottom third of the Brookings list, Syracuse failed to rebound because it did the conventional things to draw the middle class back into the city. It built a glamorous new convention center and opened a new art museum. It encouraged entrepreneurs to develop restaurants and jazzy new boutique venues in old historic districts. It supported gentrification of architecturally distinctive neighborhoods. But these were cosmetic applications to the face of a dying city. Syracuse failed to touch the cancer that was growing and destroying it from the inside—its failing public school system. Virtually every major report on the urban crisis in America has pointed to the necessity of restoring safe neighborhoods and good schools. But you don't get one without the other. You don't get good neighborhoods or attract new firms to a city with bad schools. And you don't get good schools by simply pouring money into institutions that have become repositories of the city's poorest citizens.

But that's what schools in Syracuse and many cities had become at the end of the twentieth century, and money was seen as the "solution" to disastrous educational outcomes. The mayor's reelection report card, "Syracuse Is the Shining Light," noted that funding had increased 25 percent from 2001 to 2006, and listed this among the city's major achievements. But the report card said nothing about the high failure rates of Syracuse students on state math and reading exams.[7] Even with enormous increases in funding, salaries for teachers in Syracuse and other urban systems were far below those in affluent suburban schools where teaching conditions were better.[8]

Teacher turnover rates were also highest in urban schools. As a rule, good teachers do not want to work in schools with high concentrations of poverty because they face insurmountable odds. Children who are undernourished and in poor health, who don't get regular checkups for physical, dental, or eye care, whose families are frequently evicted, leading to higher rates of absenteeism, who are kept at home to mind younger children because parents or guardians are working, who have been arrested, who join gangs, intimidate other students, abuse drugs, and threaten teachers—these are not the kinds of students likely to perform well on mandated state tests or succeed in a college-prep curriculum. Many such children are unable to read at anything approaching grade level. A report by the Public Policy Institute of California showed that the average reading level of tenth graders in high-poverty schools is about the same as that of fifth graders in the most affluent schools.[9]

Funds to put health clinics in urban schools, to pay teachers a premium for teaching in high-poverty areas, to invest in early childhood education, after-school programs, and summer classes, and to provide vouchers for more stable housing are desperately needed and are money well spent.[10] These steps will ameliorate the conditions in urban schools, but they will not provide educational opportunities equal to those of children in suburban schools. Schools in cities like Syracuse that have essentially become segregated institutions for the poor cannot be equalized solely by pumping more dollars into them. Syracuse already spends more per pupil than does Raleigh, but its results for poor and black children are shameful in comparison.

What Raleigh did—and what cities like Syracuse should have done—was to break down the invisible wall between city and suburbs to ensure that every school had a healthy mix of children by race and socioeconomic class. In the merged Raleigh–Wake County school system, no schools had the failure rates that were common in Syracuse. Revitalization in Syracuse failed because most of its schools were identified as repositories for minorities and the poor. No matter how many new convention centers might be built, the middle class was unlikely to be drawn to a city where it could not, in good conscience, send its children to public school. Neighborhoods would not flourish there, technology firms would not locate there, and the so-called "creative class" would not become urban pioneers there.

Syracuse tried at one point to balance its schools racially and economically. In the late 1960s, under the force of a state law, Syracuse adopted a plan to desegregate its city schools. When the plan was fully implemented in the early 1970s, some city high schools, like Hamilton, went from 90 percent white to 50 percent black practically overnight. Schools and teachers were unprepared for such massive change, and riots broke out in two high schools. If racial desegregation had occurred on a metropolitan basis and had included the county school population, which was 92 percent white, the proportion of black and poor children in each school would have dropped to the single digits.

Desegregation would not have swamped the resources of any school or upset each school's ability to peacefully absorb a small proportion of new students.

While some white flight began with the onset of the desegregation plan in Syracuse, the major emptying out of the city by middle-class whites did not come until the 1970s, after a series of Supreme Court decisions forced desegregation on northern cities. Though it is now difficult for many to recall, for more than two decades after the 1954 *Brown* decision, segregation was widely regarded solely as a southern problem. Racial apartheid —laws promulgating separate schools for blacks and whites— was a southern creation, and virtually all the cases seeking to overturn segregated schools that reached the Supreme Court came from southern and border states. In the view of pious northerners, it was the South that had a problem with the separation of people by race, not the North.

The Court struck down those apartheid laws in the *Brown* decision, but only minimal desegregation took place until 1968, when the Court lost its patience and said it was no longer enough to simply allow black students to apply to white schools but that school boards had an affirmative obligation to desegregate schools. In *Green v. County School Board of New Kent County,* a rural school district south of Richmond, the Court ruled that the School Board must "come forward with a plan that promises realistically to work, and . . . to work now."[11] It was a major shift that turned desegregation from a trickle to a flood in many southern school districts.

Three years later, the Court went further, ordering county-wide busing to achieve desegregation in Charlotte, North Carolina. Charlotte and its surrounding Mecklenburg County had merged years earlier for reasons having nothing to do with desegregation. Under a minimalist integration plan, its schools had remained largely segregated, although now within one school district. Two thirds of the black students attended all-black schools. District Judge James B. McMillan's remedy divided the county school zones into pie-shaped wedges extending from the center of the city outward into the suburbs, so that every school would be racially balanced. Blacks made up 29 percent of the total school population, and under the new busing plan black enrollment within each school would range from 9 to 38 percent. Although the Fourth Circuit Court of Appeals struck down McMillan's busing plan, it was later upheld by the Supreme Court, which accepted not only the need for widespread busing between Charlotte and its suburbs but also the principle of achieving a reasonable racial balance in all schools throughout the county.[12]

The Supreme Court first ordered school desegregation in the North in a 1973 case that arose in Denver. It was also the Court's first ruling that began to erase the distinction between de jure and de facto discrimination. While no law in Denver separated the races (de jure segregation), the actual or de facto segregation in schools was the result of manipulation of student attendance zones, school site selection, and feeder patterns designed to keep blacks out of white schools. It was the intent of those policies that mattered, not the language. Government policies in the North were having the same effect as the laws in the South that had been struck down—they were establishing dual school systems, and therefore they required the same remedy.[13] But the remedy in Denver's case was restricted to the city's school system, and did not include the suburbs.

The Tragic Case of Detroit

The following year the Court heard an appeal to reverse the metropolitan desegregation plan in Detroit, which would have integrated the city's students with those in suburban schools, based on a logic similar to that in the Charlotte case. But the Court refused to apply the logic of the Charlotte decision to Detroit and instead struck down the Detroit desegregation plan. It was a tragic decision that in many ways sealed the fate of cities in the North. Arguably, more than any other single factor, the Detroit ruling ensured that black and poor children in cities like Syracuse would continue to be segregated and that city school systems would have no power to merge with suburban schools.

The Supreme Court overturned Detroit's metropolitan desegregation plan by a narrow 5–4 decision. But for one vote, a middle-class exodus would have been greatly curtailed. Some families would have continued to depart for the suburbs no matter what the Supreme Court decided. But other parents would have thought, why abandon the city if our children can attend the same schools as those in the suburbs, which will be equally integrated on a much fairer basis than an integration plan restricted to the city only. In fact, that is what happened in Raleigh, where city property values rose after the merger with the county schools.

Though Detroit was a much larger city than Syracuse, its history of racial segregation was similar. The state of Michigan fixed the city's boundaries in 1926 when it adopted restrictive annexation laws limiting expansion of the city and ensuring that postwar growth would occur in legally separate suburbs. Detroit was only 4 percent black in 1930, but President Roosevelt's 1941 executive order forbidding racial discrimination in defense industries brought tens of thousands of blacks to Detroit in the 1940s and thereafter. Restrictive covenants, white preferences, and discrimination by real estate brokers kept them within clearly defined black neighborhoods in the inner city.

By 1970, the population of Detroit was 40 percent black, and its school-age population was 52 percent black. Detroit obtained $360 million in federal funds for a model schools program in the 1960s, but it did little to change opportunities for African American children. In litigation that led to the Detroit decision, an NAACP legal team contended that the apartheid housing system was due to deliberate policies. Attorneys for the plaintiffs documented dozens of actions by city officials to maximize segregation by redrawing attendance boundaries and by establishing transfer policies that allowed white children to escape from predominantly black schools.[14] They also showed that the state of Michigan had taken action to unlawfully maintain segregated schools when the legislature nullified a plan to integrate Detroit's schools in the spring of 1971.[15]

The case was heard by Federal District Court Judge Stephen Roth, a conservative among Michigan Democrats whose decision surprised many. Judge Roth left no doubt that he was convinced of the evidence:

> The city of Detroit is a community generally divided by racial lines. Residential segregation within the city and throughout the large metropolitan area is substantial, pervasive and of long standing. Black citizens are located in separate and distinct areas within the city and are not generally to be found in the suburbs. While the racially unrestricted choice of black persons and economic factors may have played some part in the development of this pattern of residential segregation, it is, in the main, the result of past and present practices and customs of racial discrimination, both public and private, which have and do restrict the housing opportunities of black people. On the record, there can be no other finding.

In light of the eventual reversal of this opinion, it is important to note that Judge Roth's findings were not restricted to the city of Detroit. He also pointed to segregative policies pursued at the state and federal level that created a deep divide between northern cities and their suburbs. His finding that these government policies constituted a form of de jure segregation throughout the metropolitan area broke new ground:

> Government actions and inactions at all levels, Federal, State, and local, have combined with those of private organizations, such as loaning institutions and real estate associations and brokerage firms, to establish and to maintain the pattern of residential segregation through the Detroit metropolitan area. The policies pursued by both government and private persons and agencies have a continuing and present effect upon the complexion of the community . . . as we know the choice of residence is a relatively infrequent affair. For many years FHA and VA openly advised and advocated the maintenance of "harmonious" neighborhoods, that is, racially and economically harmonious. The conditions created continue.[16]

Roth concluded that a desegregation plan limited to the city of Detroit simply would not work. Its public schools were approaching a two-thirds black enrollment. Integration solely within the city would not achieve a fair balance of white and black students, and, he predicted, it would lead to more white flight and ever-greater concentrations of minority and poor pupils.

Even before Judge Roth announced a remedy in 1972, the Detroit School Board voted not to contest his finding of de jure segregation. The board urged Roth to develop a metropolitan remedy that would include busing across city-suburban boundaries. Roth eventually approved a plan that divided the metropolitan area into 17 moderately sized school districts, each containing a strong majority of white suburban students and a slice of the increasingly black central city. Each of the districts would be about 25 percent black. The faculty of each school would be at least 10 percent black and the student enrollment would be between 20 and 31 percent black.[17] It was remarkably similar to the remedy the Supreme Court had approved in Charlotte, where the city and its suburbs were divided into pie-shaped zones.

Immediately, opponents wildly exaggerated the amount of busing that the Detroit plan would require. Many newspapers uncritically published reports saying that more than 300,000 pupils out of 780,000 in all seventeen districts would be bused, neglecting to mention that most of these students in both the city and its suburbs were already being bused short distances to school. A more realistic estimate would entail the busing of about 40,000 additional black students and a similar number of whites.[18]

Suburban districts opposing the plan joined the State of Michigan in an appeal. A three-justice panel of the Sixth Circuit Court of Appeals upheld Judge Roth's ruling. The plaintiffs then filed for a rehearing before the full Appeals Court, which in 1973 also affirmed Roth's finding that unconstitutional violations were committed by state officials and agreed the metropolitan area desegregation plan was the only feasible solution.

The U.S. Supreme Court heard the case in 1974 and reversed Roth's decision by a 5 to 4 vote. The majority disagreed that state policies and the history of racial residential segregation stemming in part from actions of government agencies constituted de jure segregation that justified a metropolitan desegregation remedy. The Court ruled that such a remedy could be justified only if it were shown that suburban school districts had barred black students from attending suburban schools. Hence, the desegregation remedy could be applied only to schools within the city of Detroit, which had committed de jure violations by gerrymandering school boundaries and adopting other discriminatory policies.

The Supreme Court's majority opinion also argued that the consolidation of suburban and city school districts would be disruptive and "give rise to an array of other problems in financing and operating this new school system." It raised questions about the status of school boards in the consolidated districts and asked who would determine curricula, "establish attendance zones, purchase school equipment, locate and construct new schools, and indeed attend to all the myriad day-to-day decisions that are necessary to school operations?" The Court's majority did not acknowledge that New York City and other large school districts had solved such problems, and that Charlotte had done so under the Court's own order.[19]

Justice Byron White, writing the dissenting opinion joined by Justices William Brennan, William Douglas, and Thurgood Marshall, concluded "that deliberate acts of segregation and their consequences will go unremedied, not because a remedy would be infeasible or unreasonable in terms of usual criteria governing school desegregation cases, but because the remedy would cause what the Court considers to be undue administrative inconvenience to the State." White was "even more mystified as to how the Court can ignore the legal reality that the constitutional violations, even if occurring locally, were committed by government entities for which the State is responsible and that it is the state that must respond to the command of the Fourteenth Amendment." The dissent concluded that a metropolitan remedy is "well within . . . the powers of the State." In his concurring dissent, Justice Marshall proved correct: "Because of the already high and rapidly increasing percentage of Negro students in the Detroit system, as well as the prospect of white flight, a Detroit-only plan simply has no hope of achieving actual desegregation."[20]

The Nixon Court

The narrow decision to quash the Detroit metropolitan desegregation plan was rendered by five judges, four of whom President Nixon had appointed: Warren Burger, Harry Blackmun, Lewis F. Powell Jr., and William Rehnquist. While Nixon stated publicly that his intention was to appoint strict constructionists without any test of their views on particular cases, his private transcripts revealed that he applied a severe test to each of the nominees he considered: the candidate must be against busing. Nixon's practice of taping his White House conversations gave a rare glimpse into how he packed the Supreme Court against busing. On September 29, 1971, the morning after Judge Roth announced his decision, Nixon was meeting with his top aide and chief of staff, Bob Haldeman, who told him that the Detroit decision ordered "forced busing," a term Nixon often used, and then said: "Wait until you get your Court, maybe you can get it turned around."

With the opportunity to appoint two justices that fall, Nixon considered more than a score of nominees. He eventually appointed Rehnquist and Powell. Fearing that his earlier record as head of the Richmond School Board during its resistance to desegregation and his membership in an all-white country club would derail his nomination, Powell hesitated to accept. Rehnquist, who was then an assistant attorney general in the Justice Department, had been accused of harassing black voters at the polls in Phoenix, Arizona, in 1968, and in 1952 when he was a clerk for Supreme Court Justice Robert Jackson he had recommended against the *Brown* desegregation decision.[21] "Separate but equal" facilities were all that the Constitution required, Rehnquist had written in a memorandum. Under questioning during his Senate confirmation hearings, Rehnquist admitted he had written the memo but claimed that it did not reflect his own position; he was merely summarizing Jackson's position. A law clerk who served with Rehnquist at the time testified that these were Rehnquist's own views. In the end, both nominees were confirmed.

Nixon repeatedly applied the anti-busing test to any candidate under consideration for the Court. In one exchange with Haldeman while they were waiting for Attorney General John Mitchell to enter the Oval Office, Nixon said, "Whatever happens in the [1972] election, we will have changed the Court. I will have named four and, Potter Stewart becomes the swing man. He's a God damn weak reed, I must say. But if we can get him on board, we'll have the Court." Soon after Mitchell took his seat, Nixon turned to the business of Supreme Court appointments, and to ensuring that conversations about his real criteria would be kept private: "With regard to this Court thing, John, of course, you and I have got to decide who we tell, so we'll get all the input we can. But just the two of us will talk." Then Nixon cut to the real litmus test: "I don't care if he's a Democrat or a Republican . . . within the definition of conservative, he must be against busing, and against forced housing integration [through vouchers]. Beyond that, he can do what he pleases."

Nixon was making sure that he would not have to ask any nominee about his stand on busing, while directing Mitchell and key aides to apply that test to any potential appointment they brought to the president's desk. Because of the possible retirement of a second justice, Mitchell suggested to Nixon that he might make a "double play."

Nixon: Well, even then I don't want a liberal.

Mitchell: Oh no, no.

Nixon: I don't want a liberal.

Mitchell: Absolutely not.

Nixon: I just feel so strongly about that. I mean, when I think what the busing decisions have done to the South, and what it could do with de facto busing [in the North].

Mitchell: I agree.

Before Mitchell left, Nixon underlined his instructions once again: "I want you to have a specific talk with whatever man you consider. And I have to have an absolute commitment from him on busing and integration. I really have to. Go out and tell 'em that we totally respect his right to do otherwise, but if he believes otherwise, I don't want to appoint him to the Court."[22]

Nixon got the Court he wanted. The four justices he appointed —replacing liberal judges of the Warren Court, including Chief Justice Earl Warren himself, along with Abe Fortas, Hugo Black, and John Marshall Harlan—radically changed the direction of the U.S. Supreme Court and provided the majority to stop desegregation at the city line in the North. The Warren Court had ordered desegregation of city and suburbs in Charlotte in 1968, but Nixon's Court refused to do so in 1974 in Detroit.

Ironically, it was one of Nixon's appointees, Lewis F. Powell Jr., who made one of the sharpest attacks on the false logic of the distinction the Court had drawn between de jure and de facto segregation. In his opinion in the Denver case, "concurring in part and dissenting in part," Powell wrote:

We must recognize that the evil of operating separate schools is no less in Denver than in Atlanta. In my view we should abandon a distinction which long since has outlived its time, and formulate constitutional principles of national rather than merely regional application . . . I would not . . . perpetuate the *de jure/de facto* distinction nor would I leave to petitioners the initial tortuous effort of identifying "segregative acts" and deducing "segregative intent." I would hold, quite simply, that where segregated public schools exist within a school district, there is a prima facie case that the duly constituted public authorities are sufficiently responsible to warrant imposing upon them a nationally applicable burden to demonstrate that they nevertheless are operating a genuinely integrated school system.

Powell went on to note "in decreeing remedial requirements for the Charlotte-Mecklenburg school district," the Court "dealt with a metropolitan, urbanized area in which the basic causes of segregation were generally similar to those in all sections of the country." However, in the Detroit decision Powell contradicted himself, voting with the majority against a metropolitan remedy on the grounds that suburban school districts had not been guilty of de jure discrimination. Powell feared that busing on the scale required in Detroit would be too disruptive, and he was especially reluctant to order busing of elementary school children.[23]

Justice William Brennan tried to win Powell over, noting that he and Powell agreed on the illogic of the de jure/de facto distinction. In a memo circulated to Powell and the other justices, however, Brennan recognized that while they could agree on the causes of segregation, they could not agree on the remedy:

> Although Lewis [Powell] and I seem to share the view that de facto segregation and de jure segregation (as we have previously used those terms) should receive like constitutional treatment, we are in substantial disagreement, I think, on what that treatment should be. Unlike Lewis, I would retain the definition of the "affirmative duty to desegregate" set forth in our prior cases. Lewis's approach has the virtue of discarding an illogical and unworkable distinction, but only at the price of a substantial retreat from our commitment of the past twenty years to eliminate all vestiges of state-imposed segregation in the public schools. In my view, we can eliminate the distinction without cutting back on our commitment, and I would gladly do so.[24]

But Powell voted with the Nixon majority in the Detroit case. Only a week after the Supreme Court overruled Judge Roth, the

U.S. House of Representatives passed a bill placing restrictions on busing to achieve school integration. Although it was not as strong as the bill Nixon had earlier endorsed, *The New York Times* noted that the Court's decision "banning the busing of children across school district lines for desegregation in Detroit had made it easier for the House to accept" an anti-busing bill. Senator John L. McClellan of Arkansas, in a hearing on equal educational opportunity, accused the federal government of "monumental hypocrisy" in forcing southern schools to desegregate to a level that was intolerable in the North. Mixing sarcasm with extensive citations of "flagrant violations," McClellan assailed both Democratic and Republican administrations for failing to act against what he called officially sanctioned school segregation in the North.[25]

McClellan and Nixon both read the polls, and they knew a major shift in attitudes about school desegregation was under way. The North had no Jim Crow laws, but it had plenty of racism. In 1942 only 38 percent of white Americans agreed that whites and blacks should go to the same schools. It was not until 1956, two years after the Supreme Court outlawed school segregation in the South, that 50 percent of whites agreed that both races should attend the same schools, rising to 86 percent by 1972 and 96 percent by the end of the century.[26]

While there was wide agreement on the principle of racially integrated schools, there was bitter disagreement about how it should be achieved. In the 1960s, polls asking whites whether the government should intervene to bring about school integration revealed a major split between attitudes in the North and the South. In 1966, when most in the North saw resistance to school integration as primarily a southern problem, 60 percent of northern whites agreed that "Washington should see to it that white and black children go to the same schools"; only 35 percent of those in the South held this view. By 1976, two years after the Supreme Court banned metropolitan busing in Detroit, northern support for government intervention to integrate schools dropped to the same low level as in the South.[27]

Although Black Power advocates argued against integration and in favor of keeping blacks in their neighborhood schools, a majority of African Americans continued to agree that government should intervene to bring about integration. But even black support dipped from 86 to 76 percent after the Supreme Court's Detroit decision. Asked specifically about cross-district busing in 1974, the year of much media coverage of the Detroit decision, 63 percent of blacks said they were in favor of "busing black and white children from one school district to another" to achieve racially desegregated schools, compared with only 15 percent of whites.[28]

George C. Wallace, the segregationist governor of Alabama, playing to white anxieties about integrated housing and desegregated schools, made an impressive showing in a number of Democratic presidential primaries in 1972, earning more than 40 percent of the vote in Maryland, Michigan, and Wisconsin.[29] By the mid-1970s even liberal Democrats, especially those dependent on white suburban votes, were condemning busing. Senator Joseph R. Biden Jr., Democrat from Delaware at the time, attracted other liberals to an amendment that would "prevent Federal bureaucrats from ordering busing." Senator Jacob Javits, a liberal New York Republican who would not go along, said of those who did, "They're scared to death of busing."[30]

Earlier, Senator Abraham Ribicoff of Connecticut had also risen to speak against the hypocrisy of condemning segregation only in the South:

Unfortunately, as the problem of racial isolation has moved north of the Mason-Dixon line, many northerners have bid an evasive farewell to the hundred-year-old struggle for racial equality. Our motto seems to have been "Do to southerners what you do not want to do to yourself." Good reasons have always been offered, of course, for not moving vigorously ahead in the North as well as the South. First, it was that the problem was worse in the South. Then the facts began to show that was no longer true. We then began to hear the de facto–de jure refrain. Somehow residential segregation in the North was accidental or de facto and that made it better than the legally supported de jure segregation in the South. It was a hard distinction for black children in totally segregated schools in the North to understand, but it allowed us to avoid the problem.[31]

Justice Powell took pleasure in quoting Senator Ribicoff, who, like himself, also recognized the unfairness of applying a different standard in the North than in the South. But Nixon's test for his Supreme Court appointees had triumphed. As Haldeman had predicted, Nixon got his Court. And the Nixon Court never approved metropolitan desegregation in the North.[32]

6 | What Should We Hope For?

Four years after Supreme Court Justice Lewis Powell Jr. supplied the deciding vote that quashed the Detroit metropolitan desegregation plan, he shifted his view closer to the position of the liberal minority on the Court on the issue of affirmative action. Powell again provided the deciding vote in a 5–4 decision that allowed colleges and universities to use race as a factor in college admissions.[1] It is tempting to speculate that he might have voted differently on metropolitan desegregation if he had remained on the Court long enough to see the success of city-suburban busing in Raleigh and Charlotte.

In 1954 virtually all members of the United States Senate and the House of Representatives from the Old South had signed the "Southern Manifesto" in opposition to the Supreme Court's decision outlawing school segregation in *Brown v. Board of Education.* Despite this strong initial resistance, large-scale metropolitan desegregation was eventually achieved in the South. Would the anti-busing frenzy have resulted in a "Northern Manifesto" if the Supreme Court had ordered school desegregation in metropolitan Detroit? Would the Supreme Court have voted differently or would public reaction to metropolitan desegregation have been different if we had known then what we know now?

Two generations of children have grown up since large-scale desegregation began in the South. Three decades of research after the 1974 Detroit decision revealed much about the costs of continued segregation as well as the potential benefits of racially and economically balanced schools. One question raised in the Detroit case has been answered. White flight from northern cities was, without a doubt, hastened by the Detroit decision. In Syracuse, 98 percent of all black residents of Onondaga County lived within the city, though countywide they made up only 9 percent of the total population of 460,000. If Syracuse had desegregated on a countywide basis as Raleigh did, so that poor and minority students were spread throughout the system, integration would most likely have proceeded peacefully and effectively. But because desegregation was restricted to the city, it was extremely difficult to racially balance schools for long. And for most white parents, it was not a wrenching decision to move to the suburbs in order to avoid sending their children to low-performance schools that rapidly became overloaded with poor and minority pupils.

In Raleigh, by contrast, where schools were fairly balanced throughout the county, and continuously rebalanced, few families moved to another metropolitan area to avoid desegregation, and private school enrollment increased by only a few percentage points after the merger, even though the proportion of blacks in Wake County was nearly three times that in Syracuse's Onondaga County. Virtually all middle- and upper-class families in Raleigh and Wake County continued to enroll their children in the public schools. When schools reflect a fair balance of all children, parents feel their children are safe and do not believe the norms underlying a good school are going to be upset. Polls of Wake County parents strongly supported that view. In 2006, 94 percent of parents agreed or strongly agreed with the statement: "My child's school provides a high-quality educational program." Ninety-six percent said it was "a safe place to learn."[2]

The norms of a good school are shaped more by the children who come through the door than the dollars spent on books, buildings, laboratories, teacher salaries, or other traditional measures of school quality. This was the finding of a landmark study of equal educational opportunity by James Coleman in 1966.[3] The largest survey of schools up to that time, it was funded by Congress with the expectation that it would reveal wide disparities in traditional spending measures between black and white schools. The differences it found were not as large as expected, due partly to efforts in the South to provide equal facilities for black schools, as a way to undergird the "separate but equal" doctrine. Coleman's research revealed that what really counted was who you went to school with. This finding, which astonished both Congress and most educators, was initially disputed by many and ignored by others.[4] But Coleman's central finding has since been reconfirmed in many studies: "The social composition of the student body is more highly related to achievement, independent of the student's own social background, than is any other school factor."[5]

Simply put, Coleman found that the achievement of both poor and rich children was depressed by attending a school where most children came from low-income families. More important to the goal of achieving equal educational opportunity, he found that the achievement of poor children was raised by attending a predominantly middle-class school, while the achievement of affluent children in the school was not harmed. This was true even if per-pupil expenditures were the same at both schools. No research over the last forty years has overturned Coleman's finding that most of the achievement difference between schools was due to the family backgrounds of students attending those schools, and that the high tide of achievement in a predominantly middle-class school raises all boats.

Why is this so? Why should it matter who is sitting next to a child as long as the child pays attention, works hard, and does her homework? If we are only talking about two pupils, it doesn't matter if one is wealthy and the other is from the projects, or if one is white and the other black. But if we are talking about a school where 70 or 80 percent of those a child is likely to sit next to are from the projects, it makes a huge difference. The fact that poor parents are much more likely to have dropped out of school, to speak nonstandard English, to be unable to provide regular medical care or homework supervision doesn't change even if their children transfer to a school where most of their classmates are middle class. These poor children may still have bad teeth and start school without having heard bedtime stories. They may enter first grade with a smaller Standard English vocabulary and may have more trouble learning to read.[6] But many other things will change for these poor children in a school that is fairly balanced across lines of socioeconomic class, like those in Wake County.

The norms of behavior, the language spoken, and the expectations of teachers will be vastly different. Gangs will not run the schools. The learning curve will be higher. Students and teachers will no longer have to confront a culture that ridicules traditional school achievement. Sloppy and vulgar speech are less likely to be tolerated. The vocabularies of poor children will grow as they interact with advantaged classmates. More will learn to read sooner. Teachers will not be overburdened and burned out, as they often are in high-poverty schools. Children will not have an easy time ducking homework assignments. Better teachers with even higher expectations for what counts as good work will be attracted to these high-performing schools.

Teacher turnover will decrease. Poor children in predominantly middle-class schools may not achieve at the level of students who start school far more advantaged than they are. But more poor children will reach grade level, and they will graduate in far greater numbers.

Those who believe the Supreme Court was right to halt metropolitan desegregation plans in the North often portray such plans as unnecessary and burdensome. They denigrate them as utopian schemes of social engineering that freedom-loving Americans should resist. They point to highly publicized inner-city academies like KIPP (Knowledge Is Power Program) that have achieved powerful results without "forced busing." These are good schools, and they have been successful partly for the same reason that Raleigh has: they changed the norms that are operative in most inner-city schools. They did it by setting requirements for longer school days (starting as early as 6:30 a.m. and often not ending until 5 p.m.), Saturday classes, mandatory summer school, and behavioral contracts with parents.

A similarly successful private school I visited in Harlem required that a guardian accompany the student applicant for a full-day visit to the school. On completion of the visit, the prospective student had to write an essay explaining what the school was about and why he or she wanted to attend. Students and parents who find out about such schools and commit the time and effort to apply and abide by these stringent rules are a small subset of impoverished inner-city families. They tend to be children from stable homes with the most motivated parents (or a single parent) who enforce strong beliefs in educational achievement and who back up school norms governing good behavior and academic effort. When drawn to a KIPP academy or a similar school with other like-minded parents, they reinforce those norms. They confirm Coleman's findings that parental background factors are critical to establishing a context for higher achievement. But such schools are few in number—islands of hope in a sea of poverty, as a recent report funded by the Gates Foundation confirmed.[7]

In 2004 KIPP and other charter schools enrolled only 2 percent of all public school students in the nation. Many of them did no better than other public schools in improving the achievement of children in high-poverty schools. In Washington, D.C., a city that enrolled 26 percent of its pupils in charter schools in 2005—one of the highest rates in the nation—only 12 percent of its eighth grade students reached proficiency in reading and 7 percent in math.[8] No city like Washington or Syracuse with high concentrations of schools in poverty has been able to replicate the success of KIPP and similar exceptional schools on a city-wide basis. By creating fairly balanced schools on a countywide basis, Wake County changed the norms in *all* schools attended by poor students.

Wake Is Not the Only One

While Wake has been a leader in closing the achievement gap, metropolitan desegregation has also markedly improved academic achievement of poor and minority pupils in other districts. The most successful desegregation occurred in the South, especially in the countywide school districts that are common in many southern states, and later through city-suburban mergers. Massive resistance and delaying tactics blocked desegregation for more than a decade: only 2 percent of black students had entered white schools in the South by 1964. But by 1988 southern schools were the most integrated in the nation, with 44 percent of black students attending schools that were majority white, compared with only 23 percent of blacks in the Northeast. Equally important, in 2003 there were three times as many poor minority students attending affluent schools (those with less than 10 percent of their students receiving free and reduced lunch) in the South as there were in the Northeast.[9]

Charlotte's school merger with Mecklenburg County in 1971, though court-ordered, achieved outcomes that were nearly as remarkable as Raleigh's. Being one of the earliest metropolitan plans, it was also one of the most studied. The first few years of integration saw considerable turbulence, and ten high schools closed for short periods due to racial tension. But eventually, significant gains were made. Roslyn Arlen Mickelson's fifteen-year study showed not only that desegregation benefited both black and white students but that students who attended desegregated schools for more years accrued more benefits: "The more time both black and white students spend in desegregated elementary schools, the higher their standardized test scores in middle and high school and the higher their track placements in secondary schools."[10]

Chattanooga, Tennessee, offers an interesting parallel with both Syracuse and Raleigh. It was a declining industrial city of about the same size as Syracuse that had tried the usual paths to revival. It had cleaned up downtown, torn down substandard housing, and built a $45 million aquarium on the banks of the Tennessee River in hopes of becoming a "destination city." But this was not enough to reverse the decline. After years of shrinking school enrollments and mushrooming expenses, with some of the lowest test scores in the state, the city's business and civic leadership came together to convince voters that excellent public schools were the missing link in their chain of hopes for Chattanooga. As in Raleigh, they feared Chattanooga was becoming the hole in a donut of metropolitan prosperity. "We need to be concerned about the overall school system because it's related to our economic health," said Ronald O'Neal, owner of a large plumbing and manufacturing company and president of the Hamilton County School Board. "That's what draws companies in. They want to know about our schools."

Chattanooga's School Board decided to follow Nashville and Knoxville on the road to merger with the suburbs. It wasn't easy. The city schools' 155,000 pupils were 65 percent black, while schools in Hamilton County were 95 percent white. There were fears of massive busing and loss of teaching jobs in a merged system. After two years of debate, the city chose merger in 1997 by a referendum vote of 22,694 to 19,044. For three years after the merger, as the consolidated system designed new approaches to teaching and learning in more diverse schools, test scores were nearly flat. But by 2000 Chattanooga–Hamilton County became one of the fastest-improving school systems in the state. Over the next seven years the dropout rate was cut in half, and 75 percent of all students graduated from high school in 2007. Passing rates for black children in grades three through eight rose to 81 percent in math and 83 percent in reading by that year, while rates for low-income students were 83 percent in math and 85 percent in reading. "The merger brought new energy not just in the schools, but in the community," said Daniel Challener, president of the Public Education Foundation. "It was a catalyst for greater community involvement and investment."[11]

Louisville, Kentucky, like Charlotte, had once operated separate schools for whites and blacks. It had been ordered in 1975 to develop a metropolitan desegregation plan for schools in the city and Jefferson County. Black achievement rose and dropout rates fell. President Ronald Reagan's secretary of education, Terrel H. Bell, called Jefferson County's desegregation plan the most successful in the country. In 2001, after a federal court declared Jefferson County "unitary," or free of the vestiges of past discrimination, the district acted to prevent resegregation. A study of 38 districts that had been declared "unitary" showed that in fact significant resegregation had occurred in most districts.

Charlotte was one of them. Though most Charlotte schools remained racially balanced, resegregation increased when Charlotte adopted a neighborhood school policy after being declared unitary in 2002. In the South overall, the percentage of blacks in majority-white schools dropped from a peak of 44 percent in 1988 to 28 percent in 2005.[12]

Louisville and Jefferson County voluntarily adopted a managed choice plan to maintain racial balance among its 97,000 students, which were one third black overall. As in Raleigh, parents could list their preferences, but assignments were tailored to sustain a black enrollment of at least 15 percent but no more than 50 percent. Jefferson County schools continued to make progress. More than 80 percent of black and 77 percent of white graduates strongly agreed that it was important for "my long-term success in life" to have attended desegregated schools.[13]

But in 2007 the Supreme Court struck down Jefferson County's voluntary plan on the grounds that assignment by race was unconstitutional now that Louisville and Jefferson County had jointly eliminated their previous race-based school systems. The Court's decision, by a 5 to 4 vote, did permit taking race into account within narrow limits, such as drawing attendance zones for new schools or allocating resources for special programs, but it eliminated most voluntary desegregation programs based on race. That decision may lead Louisville and other districts to adopt Raleigh's policy of balancing schools by family income rather than race, as Fairfax County, Virginia, has done.[14] There is strong evidence to support such a policy.

Why Class and Income Trump Race

A national study of 913 high schools completed in 2005 confirmed the benefit of socioeconomically balanced schools. It found that "schools serving mostly lower-income students tend to be organized and operated differently than those serving more affluent students." The differences paralleled those in Raleigh and were traceable to four characteristics of balanced schools: higher teacher expectations, greater amounts of homework, more rigorous courses, and students' feelings of safety. Poor students in schools balanced according to income learned, on average, twice as much as those in high-poverty schools.[15]

In much of the discussion of desegregation, race is often used as a proxy for income or social class. Studies frequently refer to "poor blacks" or "low-income minorities." Such usage is understandable: blacks and minorities are disproportionately poor. But class or income trumps race as a determinant of academic achievement.[16] When black and white students of similar income and parental education are compared, most of the racial difference disappears. This is true whether one is comparing test scores or measures of behavior in school. A study of antisocial behavior calculated the frequency of noncooperative behavior, dishonesty, disobedience, and violence among twelve-year-olds. A comparison of the raw scores of all black children in the sample with all whites indicated that blacks were markedly more antisocial than whites, a thirteen-point difference. But when blacks and whites of similar social class and parental education were compared, the differences were negligible: only three points, an antisocial score of 53 for blacks and 50 for whites. The average antisocial score of the poorest children, regardless of race, was 49, but it was only 28 for children in the best-off

166

families. The real difference in school behavior was family income.[17]

Without a doubt, poor black children bear the additional disadvantage of historic discrimination because of skin color. Continued efforts to achieve racial desegregation are justified on that ground alone, although the composition of the current Supreme Court makes it highly unlikely that this argument will prevail. But when poor black children are integrated with poor whites, as happened in parts of Boston and in some rural districts in the South, neither black nor white children made gains. The real gains come from integration by class or income. In recognition of overwhelming research evidence supporting this proposition, Wake County in January 2000 became the first large school district to adopt income rather than race as the principal measure of balance. The new policy stipulated, first, that no school would be majority-poor—that is, the percentage of students eligible for free or reduced-price lunch would not exceed 40 percent. And second, no school would have more than 25 percent of its students reading below grade level.

Wake County was not abandoning hope for continued racial balance. The School Board understood that a high proportion of black and Hispanic families were poor. In 1994 nearly a third of the county's minority students read below grade level, and more than half of them received subsidized lunches, while only 15 percent of whites fell into either category. Economic integration would bring about significant racial balance as well. But by 2000 Wake was also aware that the courts were turning against racial assignment. The Fourth District Court of Appeals, which had jurisdiction over North Carolina, had recently barred the use of race as a basis for student assignments in Arlington, Virginia.

Stephen Wray, chair of the Wake School Board, explained the

board's unanimous vote for the change: "Our objective has shifted from racial diversity to one that is focused on achievement. I am comfortable with racial diversity being a by-product of this new plan. Still, it is important to understand the difference." Bill Fletcher, a conservative member of the board sensitive to complaints about busing, agreed: "The issue for me has always been educational effectiveness. That's what this policy is about, it's not social engineering."[18] The income-balance policy indeed proved to be educationally effective, and it was politically effective as well. It did not slow Wake's success in closing the racial achievement gap, but it did manage to sidestep future court challenges to Wake's long-standing racial balance plan. All poor children—whites, blacks, Asians, and Hispanics—benefited. Most importantly, it was highly effective in maintaining Wake's reputation as a place where there are no bad schools— an enormous boon for economic prosperity in the region.

While significant gains can occur solely by changing the complexion and social-class composition of students within schools, those gains can be frustrated if students are resegregated within the school by shunting poor or black children into a separate track where academic demands are low and where classes are taught by the least able teachers. Studies of racial desegregation have shown exactly that trend in some schools.[19] Wake County did not let this happen. Not only were children's expectations changed by being placed in classrooms where most of their peers were doing their homework and coming to class ready to work, but teachers' expectations were changed as well.

Wake's new culture of teaching in a data-driven system brought teachers together in teams to look at how all children at each grade-level were performing, not just the children in individual classrooms. Teachers began to question one another about why poor Hispanic boys were reading so poorly in some third grade classrooms but not in others. Principals redirected funds and extra teachers toward low-performing children, in the form of catch-up classes, extra tutoring after school, and summer programs. Wake's reputation helped the county recruit teachers from other states who knew they were not going to be assigned to inner-city schools that had become not much more than warehouses for poor, low-performing students.

That perception also attracted top administrative talent from inside and outside the system. Some principals elsewhere were willing to come to Wake as assistant principals, just to be part of a system that was making history and truly providing equal educational opportunity to all children. Wake made a point of rewarding high performance with bonuses. Teachers who demonstrated teaching excellence by passing the rigorous National Board certification program received an extra 12 percent of their base salary. By 2008 Wake County had the highest percentage of nationally certified teachers of any urban school district in the country.

What happened outside of school was just as important. The politics of maintaining public support for balanced schools was a creative and ceaseless effort. Once it adopted a policy of economic balance, Wake never stopped selling it. The leadership of the school system, especially Superintendent Bill McNeal and his successor, Del Burns, never assumed that all parents would understand the rationale or, if they did, would agree that it was worth busing children out of their neighborhood to keep schools integrated by social class. They founded the Wake Partnership—an annual conference of parents, business leaders, politicians, and principals—to explain what the system was achieving and to set new goals. It usually drew several thousand participants. A citizen task force wrote a report, "Healthy Schools," about the benefits of Wake's policy that won wide attention in the media.

Socioeconomic balance became part of the everyday language that teachers and parents used to talk about Wake's educational rationale.

Because of the influx of new families drawn to Raleigh's booming economy, new schools were opened every year, and reassignments were often necessary to keep the system in balance. Wake's wide variety of magnet schools, with their different academic emphases, gave parents a lot of choices, but inevitably some parents did not get the school they wanted for their child. The administration tried to be responsive and make adjustments, but still not all parents got a satisfactory choice. They had an opportunity to voice their complaints at public hearings held throughout the county each year. These lengthy hearings imposed a burden on the School Board, but as board member Tom Oxholm explained, "We've learned to handle this like the Department of Transportation handles new highways. Not everyone is going to like it. But it helps that everyone gets a hearing."[20] The busing policy was refined over the years to minimize complaints by reducing time on the bus and maintaining stability of enrollment within each school whenever possible.

The overwhelming majority of Wake parents were convinced that busing was worth it. Despite challenges from those who favored a neighborhood school policy, for more than three decades Wake citizens elected a School Board majority that supported balanced schools. Poll data also showed a dramatic shift nationally over those years in favor of diversity. In Gallup polls, 72 percent of white parents said in 1963 that they would not send their children to a school that was majority black. By 1990, that number had shrunk to only 34 percent. While questions that implied "forced busing" were opposed by a majority of whites, 60 percent of whites polled by Public Agenda supported "redrawing district lines to combine mostly black and mostly white districts into one school district," as Wake County did.[21]

Wake parents' confidence in the benefits of its balance policies was not shaken by debates about whether the reported academic gains of their children were as substantial as claimed. Some observers have claimed that North Carolina and other states lowered the bar on state tests to avoid penalties under the federal No Child Left Behind law that required annual testing of all public school children. But Wake set its goal of 95 percent passing before the federal law was passed, and there has been no evidence that North Carolina watered down its tests or that the remarkable closure of the test gap between black and white children in Wake was a sham. Both North Carolina and New York received above-average ratings in a recent comparison of the quality of their state testing programs.[22] Wake's pupils have done well on the SAT, which many college admissions officers regard as the gold standard of verbal and mathematical achievement. Wake students also significantly exceeded national averages on Advanced Placement tests.[23]

Teaching beyond the Test

Remarkable as Wake's success has been in shrinking the test gap between black and white pupils, it obscures other even more important achievements. As a nation, we have over-focused if not fixated on testing. But test scores explain only a small part of the reasons why people are successful in later life. In an ingenious study of life success as measured by occupational status and income, Christopher Jencks found that school grades and test scores explained only a fifth of adult success. What mattered more might be called the Woody Allen virtues: showing up

171

and sticking with it. Much of the variance in success later in life could be attributed not to grades or class standing but to whether students finished high school at all. This was true even when Jencks compared male siblings in the same family, thus controlling to some degree for family environment and genetic inheritance.[24] Poor and minority children in Wake were more likely to stay in school and graduate than poor and minority children in Syracuse or other cities where they were trapped in schools with high concentrations of poverty and low expectations.

Employers increasingly value those who can resolve conflicts and work cooperatively in diverse teams across lines of race and class in order to solve problems. Raleigh children of different races and family backgrounds have been learning to cooperate in classroom projects for two generations, and when they enter the workplace they help Raleigh's economy prosper. Some people dismiss diversity claims as liberal rhetoric, but the economist Scott Page has shown mathematically that diversity matters in firms and in political decision-making as well as in schools. Diverse perspectives "increase the number of solutions that a collection of people can find by creating different connections among the possible solutions," Page's research showed.

Mixing groups by class or race does not guarantee a diversity of views—think of the radical Weathermen whose diverse social origins could not override a rigid ideology that led to planting bombs in the 1960s. Conversely, homogeneity doesn't always lead to shared perspectives—both George W. Bush and John Kerry were affluent white graduates of Yale, and yet their political views were dramatically different. But for solving tough problems in business or politics, the best bet is to bring together large groups of diverse people with different perspectives. Page claimed that diversity trumps not only homogeneity but also ability. That is, one is likely to get a better solution to a problem from a random selection of law school graduates with diverse backgrounds and perspectives than from a group of the highest ranked whites with similar backgrounds.

Page's mathematical models showed that diverse groups were better at making predictions and that "a group's errors depend in equal parts on the ability of its members to predict and their diversity."[25] His work reminded me not only of Raleigh's classrooms, where children benefit from diversity, but also of my visits to Japanese schools, where fourth-grade children of diverse abilities would spend a whole morning in small groups trying to arrange jugs and containers of different sizes and shapes into order by volume. Teachers spent as much time discussing with the class how some groups reasoned incorrectly to arrive at the wrong answers as they did probing the methods of those who got it right. Japanese elementary schools strive to maximize the intelligence of the group, and perhaps this helps explain why their students rank among the highest in the world in mathematical achievement. Virtually no student is allowed to fail.

Children also benefit in other ways from attending diverse schools. Follow-up studies of children from inner-city schools in Boston, St. Louis, and Hartford who were voluntarily bused to suburban schools showed that they experienced major gains in social capital. Under the influence of middle-class peers, teenagers who formerly did not even understand the word "resume" began to think about how to build one. As adults, they were more likely to obtain white-collar and professional jobs, to live in integrated neighborhoods, and to have white friends.[26] The Gautreaux study of children from Chicago housing projects whose parents were given vouchers to move to the suburbs and attend schools there had fewer disciplinary problems, performed better in sports, got better jobs with better benefits, and were more likely to attend college than similar children who stayed in city schools. Robert Crain's follow-up studies of Hartford children showed that bused children had fewer difficulties with police and that teenage girls were less like to have a child before age 18.[27]

Perhaps the largest scale experiment of integration by social class and race occurred in the U.S. armed forces. Follow-up studies of thousands of poor blacks who served in Vietnam showed that they earned substantially more in civilian life than blacks from the same background who had not served. Much of this difference in outcome was attributable to the wider social networks black soldiers acquired as well as their ability to cooperate effectively across boundaries of race and class. Twice as many blacks as whites re-enlisted in order to take advantage of educational benefits within the military and the extension of the GI Bill for postservice benefits. At the end of the Vietnam War, 14 percent of all army sergeants were black. By 1990 a third of sergeants were black, as were 12 percent of commissioned officers. Colin L. Powell became chairman of the Joints Chief of Staff at a time when less than 1 percent of senior executives in the private sector were black. In the army more than 7 percent of generals were African American.

Integration was a crucial first step, but the army realized that it could not create integrated fighting units if it continued to promote only whites. When the sociologists Charles Moskos and John Sibley Butler looked closely at how the army brought black officers up through the ranks, they found it was not the result of setting artificial promotion quotas. Rather, the army set objective goals and provided compensatory educational programs so that minorities and the poor would qualify for promotion. While these programs were being developed, bottlenecks developed and fewer blacks were able to pass the qualification tests for promotion. But these problems were eventually worked out, and those who received promotions were seen by their fellow soldiers as having earned the job. This was true all the way up to the level of general. The best route to generalship was through West Point, but in 1968 only one out of a hundred plebes entering the academy were black. The army began coaching promising black and white enlisted men so that they could pass entrance tests to a special school that provided an extra year of studies to prepare students for rigorous college-level work at West Point. By 1993, 84 blacks were part of the entering class at the academy, and 40 percent of those black plebes were enlisted men who came through the army's racially integrated prep school.

Schools for the children of officers and enlisted men and women were also integrated by race and class. Nationwide, the average SAT combined score in 1994 was 741 for black schoolchildren and 940 for whites. But in schools run by the military, the gap was narrower—804 for blacks and 945 for whites—showing again that balanced schools raised the achievement of poor and minority children without depressing the achievement of whites. And significantly, the percentage of seniors in Defense Department high schools who were planning to enter college upon graduation was almost the same for both racial groups: 69 percent for whites and 64 percent for blacks.[28]

Lessons Learned

What lessons can be drawn from the Raleigh story? There are many strands woven into the tale of Raleigh's urban renaissance, among them an exceptional biracial cooperation stretching back to the Reconstruction period after the Civil War. Some of the strands are common to other modern cities of the South that also drew new industries with tax breaks in states that were less union-friendly than those in the North. But not all cities in the South or even North Carolina prospered as did Raleigh—nearby Rocky Mount and Fayetteville are two examples.

Raleigh's growth was characterized by a smart urban policy. It bulldozed less and conserved more of the attractive old city by adopting a transportation policy that ran big interstates around the city rather than through it, as did Syracuse. Raleigh was an early developer of mixed-used zoning within the city, combining attractive apartments with ground-floor retail space in a way that drew residents back into lively city streets that felt safe. It capitalized on its university assets by cooperating with the state to establish the Research Triangle Park in the 1950s.

The Research Triangle was mostly pine woods for many years. It did not really take off until after the merger of Raleigh and Wake County schools. Business leaders took an aggressive role in making the consolidation happen. They feared that the decline of Raleigh's inner city would soon become an implosion, creating a dead core that would discourage investment in the region. They knew that progressive technology-based firms would not be attracted to a dying city that projected an image of the old integration-resistant South. They wanted racially diverse, topnotch schools that would prepare the children of current employees to work in a diverse global economy and would draw talent to the area.

A 2007 Brookings Report on America's cities found that two of the major causes of decline in cities like Syracuse was that they neglected to adapt to the new electronic, information-driven global economy and they failed to overcome the extreme economic and residential isolation of the poor and minorities in the inner city. Many of these declining urban centers have a 30 percent gap on average eighth grade math and reading tests compared with test scores statewide. Of the 301 cities in the Brookings study, all of which had a population over 50,000, those in the bottom fifth on measures of economic health and growth (which included Syracuse) were also the most racially segregated.[29]

If economically and racially balanced schools are the key to revitalizing declining cities, is there a way to put that keystone back in the arch of urban renewal? Could the Detroit decision be reversed? It's unlikely. Yet the rationale for Detroit's metropolitan desegregation plan is in some ways more persuasive today than it was in 1974 when it fell one vote shy of a majority in the Supreme Court. The four justices voting in the minority thought the Michigan courts were right in finding that the patterns of segregation were caused by a web of housing discrimination and other actions by the state that maintained segregated schools—despite the fact that suburban districts did not legally bar black students from attending these predominantly white schools. The increasing concentration of segregated and impoverished schools that these justices predicted in 1974 has become a reality today in Detroit, Syracuse, and much of urban America.

In 2005 nearly eight of ten students who entered ninth grade in Detroit dropped out before graduation—the highest dropout rate of any city in the country.[30] If the Supreme Court had not struck down the Detroit plan in its 1974 *Milliken v. Bradley* decision, metropolitan desegregation would have been widely adopted throughout the rest of urban America, and cities like Syracuse would be stunningly different today. But the odds are heavily against a reversal of the *Milliken* decision, given the present composition of the Supreme Court. However, throughout our nation's history, minority opinions have later become majority opinions. It took sixty years for the Court to reverse the 1896 *Plessy v. Ferguson* decision that declared "separate but equal" schools for blacks constitutional. Perhaps one day the mounting evidence of the damage done by the Detroit decision may bring some future Court to reverse it. However, it would most likely do so not by trying to address the issue of racial diversity head-on but by upholding the principle of economic balance adopted in Raleigh.

The No Child Left Behind legislation enacted by Congress in 2001—and coming up for renewal in 2009–2010—required testing of all children in reading and mathematics in grades three through eight each year, with the aim of reaching proficiency in both subjects for all children by 2014. It was not a national test—each state designed its own tests tailored to the curriculum teachers must follow in that state. Schools were expected to make "adequate yearly progress" toward the proficiency goal not only for the school as a whole but for groups of students defined by race, poverty, language, and disability. Schools that failed for three years in a row were required to offer pupils free tutoring and the option to transfer to a school where most pupils were passing. But these were limited to within-district transfers, and in most major cities there were few seats for the thousands of poor pupils in failing schools. Nationally, only a fifth of failing students received any tutoring, and what they got was so limited as to show no significant gains in learning. The law's requirement that pupils in urban schools be taught by qualified teachers—those who were fully certified and prepared in the subjects they were assigned to teach—was largely ignored.[31]

In California alone, more than a thousand of its 9,500 schools were branded chronic failures in 2007. Most of these schools had high poverty enrollments. Nationally, more than a quarter of all public schools (25,000 of 90,000 total) failed some tests. After five years of failing, a school could be shut down under provisions of the NCLB law. About 5,000 failing schools enrolling about 2.5 million children were estimated to qualify for a shutdown as of 2008.[32]

Carmen Schroeder, the superintendent of a high-poverty district in Los Angeles, would like to close some of the worst-performing schools—59 of the 91 schools in her district have consistently failed. But she has no place to send these needy pupils.[33] Her problem is one faced by urban educators throughout America. Nationwide, 411 school districts faced sanctions for failing schools in 2008.[34] So why not offer to send children from failing schools to places where most of the successful schools are located—in the suburbs? Such a remedy would have the best political and practical chance of success if it operated as a voluntary public school voucher plan. Children in failing schools in districts where there are no available places in a successful school (or where successful schools would themselves become high-poverty schools if more classrooms were added for these children) would be offered vouchers to buy themselves a seat in a successful public school in another district.

The vouchers would need to be ample enough to provide a genuine incentive for suburban schools. They should cover the costs not only of busing but of additional teachers, counseling, tutoring, and even construction of some new schools. Each suburban school system might be offered a bonus for participation to ensure that local school taxes do not rise as a result of their accepting voucher students. And conversely, state and federal funds could be withheld from successful districts that refuse to accept vouchers from the "children left behind." If a such a carrot-and-stick approach was able to desegregate schools in the South in the 1960s and 1970s, why wouldn't it work in Syracuse and many other cities in the North today?

As in Raleigh, vouchers should offer parents from failing schools a "controlled choice." They would list their preferred schools, and the accepting districts would allocate pupils so that no school went beyond the tipping point of low-income students. Even if only 10 percent of eligible parents sought voucher transfers for their children, the benefits would be considerable. On the other hand, if massive numbers applied, the system should give priority to the neediest children, or else a lottery should be held giving an equal chance to all applicants from failing schools. The legal grounds for such a remedy would seem unassailable—they flow from the requirements set forth in existing law. It would not be a race-based program, though many minority children as well as poor white children in failing schools would be the beneficiaries. It would be a voluntary plan that does not rely on "forced" busing. It would be grounded in strong evidence from the social sciences that economically balanced schools benefit the poor without harming middle-class students.

It is important to remember that the merger of Raleigh's city schools with those in its suburbs was accomplished voluntarily, without a court order. Merger did, however, require political organization to pass enabling legislation in the state legislature, followed by approval of the county and city school boards. That could still be accomplished in Syracuse, and for the same reasons: the realization that a declining inner-city core will eventually damage the health of the suburbs and the regional economy, and the recognition of the moral imperative to provide equal educational opportunity for all children.

There has been more discussion of such matters in Syracuse in the last decade, though most of it has been limited to cost-cutting consolidation of policing, purchasing, and other services. No candidate for major political office has dared to mention merging school districts on a metropolitan basis. Existing state law is less friendly to merger in New York, and obtaining the cooperation of a multitude of suburban school districts would require extraordinary courage and political leadership. Merger and redistricting could be achieved more easily in other states, though even in Syracuse it is not impossible—if the political will could be summoned to do so.

Even without a new federal law, what could and should happen in more cities would be the kind of voluntary transfer program in which poor and minority inner-city students are bused to participating suburban districts, as Boston has done for over four decades with considerable success in its METCO program. Though such a plan was rejected when Syracuse's first black school superintendent suggested it in the mid-1970s, a voluntary one-way busing program is more likely to win acceptance today in the wake of research documenting the strong positive effects on the lives of Boston children who got on the buses for suburban schools more than forty years ago. The METCO system is still alive and well today.[35]

In the mid-1980s when I taught for two years at Hamilton High, the school had survived riots and was beginning to show some success.[36] Although white flight had taken a toll, the school retained a core of middle-class students, and grades and discipline among both black and white students had improved under a strong principal. Hamilton was Syracuse's leading high school, much like Broughton High in Raleigh. But when I went back to the school twenty years later to help teach a course in urban anthropology for two years, it was nothing like Broughton. The high school, like the city, had become increasingly poor and minority.[37]

In the years 2003 to 2005 I performed an experiment like the one I had conducted at Broughton: I asked students at Hamilton High to write a letter describing their school to a cousin who was about to move to Syracuse. The letters were devastating. Although some students felt it was still possible to get a good

181

education if you worked hard and got the right teachers, they lamented that many of the neediest students were poorly taught. They described their school as one that was "expected to be low quality and trashy." Nearly all students mentioned the degrading metal detectors they passed through each morning, although the searches offered little real protection. "They are more of a thing so that the administration can tell people they're doing it."

Such cynicism was pervasive, especially about the school's sloganeering. As one student wrote to his cousin: "As soon as you get here you will see signs all over the place with 'Community of Caring' on them. It's supposed to symbolize respect, trust, caring and responsibility. You don't find much of that here. Many aren't respectful. They talk back to teachers or bad mouth other students. There is garbage all over the halls and the bathrooms are filthy with pee all over the floors and graffiti on the walls." The school had had three principals in four years, and most teachers were afraid to discipline students or to expect much of them. One student wrote: "Well, now let's get down to business. You got it, the rules. We have rules but no one follows them. If a kid comes in drunk or high the administration doesn't care." Another offered this explanation: "Teachers come to a place like Hamilton with ambitions but once they get here they get lost in the disruptiveness of the students. Hamilton is filled with low expectations . . . If you don't expect excellence from your students they will turn in crap."

As part of their research, some students in the class made visits to suburban schools. Most had never been to such a place and could hardly believe the contrast: "As I walked through the halls of this suburban school I was in total awe of the immaculate classrooms. Everything seemed to be new and shiny. The school wasn't dark and outdated. Teachers used new technology to teach their classes and there wasn't a lack of anything. I felt a sense of jealousy, like I was being gypped." Another wrote: "White flight is no fiction. The city has been abandoned wholesale. It has had a profound effect. It has taken a pool of human potential away, and also drained money away."

A minority boy in the class had arranged to visit one of the most affluent high schools in the suburbs. But when the principal saw him interviewing students in the cafeteria about why they thought their nearly all-white school was so much better equipped than Hamilton High, he was asked to leave. He told his classmates: "I felt like I was in another country and was being expelled." The "expelled" student put the question America faces in its starkest form. In places like Syracuse, an invisible wall between city and suburbs has created two countries defined most clearly by separate educational systems—one primarily for the poor, and the other for the middle and upper classes. Many students on one side of that wall have come to believe they are losers, while those on the other side have been taught to believe they are destined for success. The choice between Raleigh and Syracuse is the choice between hope and despair, the choice between one America and two Americas.

The United States has been shaped by the twin values of liberty and equality. But for the most part liberty has trumped equality in "the land of the free and the home of the brave." In America, you can become as rich as you want, say what you want, and live as you please with fewer restrictions than any other country on earth. The power of the private purse is very great, for those who have one. We have never sought equality of condition or enforced equality of outcomes. But we have believed in the principles of equal access and equal opportunity, especially equal educational opportunity. According to the American creed, wealth does not need to be forcibly equalized because over time, if all children are provided equal educational opportunities and a chance to compete for their share of the good life, wealth will redistribute itself in a meritocratic way. Equal educational opportunity keeps the gates of promise open and prevents America from establishing impassable walls of social class and privilege.

During the colonial period, this principle was enshrined in the founding of the New England common school open to children of all social classes. It sharply differentiated America from its mother country. At the time that the common school was spreading westward across the United States, England passed its 1834 Poor Law Amendment Act, which decreed that workhouses for the poor should punish them for their debts and other failures, by separating husbands from wives, parents from children. A conservative English newspaper denounced the act, writing that it set the poor "apart like beasts in a cage, staked off from their fellow men, and regarded as beings of a different caste."[38]

It is not enough just to throw money over the wall to children in a different caste of schools. And indeed, in New York State as elsewhere, judicial decisions to remedy inequalities in funding between rich and poor districts have seldom achieved that aim once they landed in suburban-controlled state legislatures. The greatest resource for ensuring equal educational opportunity is the kind of economically balanced common school that characterizes the Raleigh–Wake County school district. The goal is not just to close the gap in test scores between black and white, rich and poor, important as that is. The goal is to provide more opportunities for people to freely associate across racial, ethnic, and economic lines. The diverse social networks that children form in the Raleigh schools promise benefits not just for themselves but, in the long run, for the nation.

All children, not just the poor, benefit from diverse perspectives and a more complex sense of what evidence and frames of analysis are useful in solving complex problems. It took courage and a bold transformation of conventional political arrangements to nourish that diversity and provide genuine equal educational opportunity in Raleigh. But merging the city and county school systems saved the city from rotting at its core and enabled a strong regional economy to thrive. A flourishing metropolitan center of arts and culture, along with world-class talent drawn to universities within Research Triangle, has made Raleigh a city of hope. Instead of turning its back on the basic promise of equal educational opportunity that America made to its poor and minority children, Raleigh embraced it. The rest of America defaults on that promise at its peril.

Epilogue

While the 1976 merger of city and county schools was a great egalitarian moment in Raleigh's history, sustaining it required creative energy and political resolve. The initial challenge was to raise achievement levels for all children and reduce the gap between black and white pupils. The second challenge was to continuously build a political coalition in favor of the busing required to maintain economically balanced and diverse schools in a rapidly expanding system.

The newly merged Wake County schools enrolled 53,000 children in 1976. By 2008 the school district had become the nineteenth largest in the nation, expanding by 6,000 pupils a year and enrolling more than 134,000 students. Raleigh's population growth was driven not only by the continued southward movement of many people from the northeastern United States but also by a rapid influx of Latino families. All of these new students, rich and poor, had to be assigned to schools, and this meant that many students who were already established in their schools had to be reassigned to keep the system in balance.

Each spring, when assignments for the following school year were announced, letters flooded into the Raleigh *News and Ob-*

server filled with protests from disgruntled parents. A mother from the affluent suburb of Cary wrote, "Wake County citizens need to rise up and say in no uncertain terms that this reassignment madness has got to stop. Why does the school system continue to interfere with the already established success of many existing schools?" She described her child's Davis Drive Elementary School as a "jewel in the crown of Wake County," despite being chronically overcrowded. "Busing in children from elsewhere" meant that Davis would "not be the same school with different children; it will be an entirely different school. No one will benefit [from] the change. Isn't excellence the goal? . . . Far more would be gained by focusing resources and attention on how best to support other schools rather than messing with success."[1]

Another Cary parent whose child was being reassigned wrote a letter along the same lines: "I am more than furious with Rosa Gill's comments about our neighborhood schools." Gill, chair of the Wake School Board, had recently noted that while the board tried to assign children to schools that were close to their homes, public schools did not legally or in any other way belong to a particular group of parents or a neighborhood but to all citizens of the county. In rebutting this point, the parent wrote, "We do not have to homogenize our schools to have excellent schools . . . Neighborhood schools worked for us, and will work for our children." Another Cary resident protested that Wake was "wasting millions on busing" because it was "fixated to the highest possible degree with the bottom 15 percent or so of students."[2]

These protests by Cary parents—objecting to the fact that low-income students at Davis Elementary would rise from 9 to 22 percent in fall 2008—got big play in the newspapers. But in fact, only a fifth of the 6,400 students reassigned throughout the county were moved to keep schools economically balanced. More than half were moved to schools closer to home, while others chose to move to magnet schools.[3]

Most parents continued to support the policy of balanced public schools. Better than nine out of ten agreed that their child was getting a "superior education" in Wake County, including voters in Cary. One of them disagreed with the mother who had complained "that students reassigned to Davis Drive Elementary will be a detriment to her jewel. Rather than welcoming families to the school, she has already counted them out . . . More disturbing is her statement that Davis Drive will not be the same school with different children . . . Excellence can be found in all schools. Unfortunately, so can prejudice." Yet another Cary parent wrote: "Bravo to the Wake County school board for addressing inequities" through its balance policies. She wished the "board members courage as they weather the complaints from a group of wealthy, lawyered-up parents."[4] The protesters turned out to be a small vocal minority, but their letters to the Raleigh *News and Observer* and the responses of those who disagreed proved that democracy was alive and well in Wake County, North Carolina.

The School Board was reelected in 2007 with little opposition and a strong majority in favor of continuing its diversity policies. Yet it struggled to maintain its previous successes in the face of spiraling growth, as more and more mobile classrooms were hauled into schoolyards. In 2008, protesting parents called for a study to determine whether busing to achieve diversity had actually helped poor students. The board was in an awkward position because the rapid increase in poor students meant that more than 30 percent of its 150 schools exceeded the 40 percent cap on poor children in any given school. Most of these schools were just over the guideline, in the 40–50 percent range, but a few had gone to 60 percent or higher, well past the tipping point of what Wake County had defined as a healthy school. Teachers in those schools faced a far greater challenge in raising achievement levels.

The board refused to raise the poverty cap, however, arguing that it would only accelerate the spread of more high-poverty schools. Instead, it attempted to bring all schools back into balance by reassigning students, despite the risk of sparking even more protests in some schools.[5] Wake County also had to face the unwelcome possibility of a tax hike to pay for services to its growing segment of needy children and for salary increases that would attract and retain the kind of teachers that had made the merger work.

As poor students, many of them Hispanic immigrants, increased from 1999 to 2007, test scores dropped. As measured by eligibility for subsidized lunches, the percentage of poor students in Wake County rose from 19 percent to 32 percent during this period, while the percentage of students passing state math and reading tests in grades three to eight fell by 9 percentage points from its high of 91 percent in 2003. The dropout rate also rose slightly.[6] But Raleigh's refusal to segregate its poor and minority students still paid big dividends. In Syracuse, where nearly three fourths of students qualified for subsidized lunches, only 29 percent of all students passed eighth grade reading. In Wake County's schools, 75 percent of poor blacks and 87 percent of blacks above the poverty line passed reading in grades 3 through 8. For Hispanics, 72 percent of poor students and 88 percent of others passed. This is especially impressive in light of the reality that some rural Latino children not only did not speak English when they came to Raleigh but also had never learned to read in their native language.

The gaps between poor and nonpoor in math were greater

than in reading, but better than 80 percent of all students in grades 3 through 8 passed math in Wake County, compared with 31 percent of eighth graders in Syracuse although there was some improvement in lower grades. In Blodgett Middle School, one of the poorest Syracuse schools, only 8 percent of eighth graders passed math and 14 percent passed reading.[7] County-wide scores in Wake were comparable to scores attained by students in the suburbs of Syracuse, where the percentage of students qualifying for subsidized lunches was less than a fourth that in Wake County. This finding suggests that a merger between Syracuse and its suburbs could have produced similar results—it could have raised the scores of the poorest students without diminishing the achievement of the affluent.

But there was no merger or any effective metropolitan approach to the problem in Syracuse. Indeed, the invisible wall between city and suburb has grown even higher in recent years. A 2006 study of Syracuse by a team from the American Institute of Architects pointed bluntly to the lack of any effective dialogue across that wall: "Urban planning policies are overlapping, inconsistent, and not enforced. Effective cooperation between city and county does not exist." As the chasm grew between affluent suburbs and an impoverished city, no one wanted to talk about, and many did not even know about, the shameful gap in test scores.[8]

Yet, this tale of two American cities is not just about test scores. It's about the kind of nation we hope to become. We should not want, nor shall we ever achieve, a nation of equal test scores or equal incomes. But we do need to decide whether we want schools segregated by race and class, or schools that provide equal educational opportunity for all children—schools where students are enriched by relationships and ways of thinking that help them break out of the boxes of race and class that our flawed history has constructed. Do we believe in a nation that welcomes all comers, provides a level playing field in all its public schools, relishes the clash of ideas, and, as a consequence, enjoys one of the highest rates of upward social mobility in the world? Raleigh's reinvention of the ideals of the American common school made it an exemplar of those dreams and hopes.

Postscript: Two Years Later

What the Epilogue suggested might happen did happen. The angry mother who said "Wake County citizens need to rise up and say in no uncertain terms that this reassignment madness has got to stop" was prophetic. In the October 2009 Wake County School Board election, candidates ran on party slates for the first time. Republicans who opposed Wake's diversity policy won all four open seats. An 8–1 majority in favor of Wake's socioeconomic balance policy flipped to a 5–4 Republican majority that began to dismantle it in favor of returning to neighborhood schools.

Fewer than 8 percent of Wake County's registered voters had turned out for the off-year, off-month election. While there was great choice among schools in Raleigh, not all parents got their first choice. Wake had become the nation's eighteenth largest school district with 143,000 students. The influx of up to six thousand pupils a year resulted in annual reassignments of some students, and the resentment of parents whose children were reassigned grew. Ironically, the old board had recently adopted a policy to do reassignments only once every three years. But that policy had not yet gone into effect. Most analysts agreed that the united Republican slate got those discontented voters to the polls. A survey of forty thousand parents by the new board after the election showed that more than 94 percent of the parents were satisfied with their child's assignment. Apparently those satisfied voters stayed home. To encourage more of them to get to the polls in the next School Board election, a new organization was formed, appropriately named Wake Up Wake!

After the new board voted to end Wake's diversity policy, School Superintendent Del Burns resigned in February 2010, saying he could no longer "in good conscience" serve them. In July, hundreds of parents, students, civil rights groups, labor leaders, and clergy marched down Fayetteville Avenue to the State Capitol to protest the board's repeal of the diversity policy. Nineteen of them were arrested for carrying their protest to the School Board later that afternoon. Protests at board meetings continued into the fall, resulting in more arrests and necessitating additional security at board meetings.[1]

The excellent reputation of Wake's high schools was called into question when the accreditation agency responsible for rating them asked the board to provide data showing that the effects of its neighborhood school policy would not result in a return to high-poverty schools that would negatively impact student achievement. The North Carolina branch of the National Association of Colored People filed a complaint under Title VI of the 1964 Civil Rights Act to block the board from moving to neighborhood school zones, threatening a cutoff of federal school aid funds. The Raleigh Chamber of Commerce and the Wake Educational Partnership, representing the business and civic leadership, urged that the board retain diversity as a factor in school assignments.[2]

Once the new board's plan to divide Wake into sixteen community school zones or districts was announced, parents began to question the reassignments that might even exceed those under the old diversity plan. Miranda Miller wrote to the Raleigh *News and Observer:* "Where will my child attend school next year? . . . Under the proposed reassignment plan, each district, and most significantly Southeast Raleigh, would undergo massive reassignment . . . causing upheaval in the lives of many students."[3]

Southeast Raleigh is the historic black district where students have been bused out of their neighborhoods for decades to achieve racial integration and economic balance in all schools. Under the new plan, many of them would be sent back. John Tedesco, a member of the Republican majority of the board, met with about a hundred members of the Raleigh-Wake Citizens Association, one of Raleigh's oldest civil rights groups, to argue that returning black children to their neighborhood schools would provide more stability for families and end the "false hope" that busing children to achieve diversity will raise their achievement. Some blacks at the meeting agreed with Tedesco, but most local black leaders opposed the return to neighborhood schools, and the predominantly black Citizens Association passed a resolution calling for the School Board to keep the diversity policy in place. A poll of Wake County teachers showed that 81 percent opposed the board's elimination of the diversity policy.[4]

In a surprise upset of the new board's policy in October 2010, one of the Republican members joined the Democrats to pass a resolution stating that "all efforts to create a zone-based assignment model will cease immediately." This did not reaffirm the former diversity policy but it seemed likely to postpone any major changes until after the next School Board election, in October 2011.[5]

In Syracuse, there were signs of rebirth in some inner-city neighborhoods, but population continued to decline while school costs rose. Proposals to consolidate governments and to merge suburban and city schools that had been put on the shelf were reopened. County legislator Tom Buckel argued that "our spending patterns reveal the cost of fragmented governments with inflexible boundaries." In a pointed comparison to Raleigh, he noted that "the largest expense in Onondaga County is for the education of 74,000 students managed by eighteen separate school districts" at a cost of $17,568 per student, while "Wake County operates a highly regarded countywide school district for 143,000 students" at a cost of $8,366 per student.

Huge gaps between city and county schools remained. In describing the "urban-suburban disconnect," the Syracuse *New Times* noted that suburban "Fayetteville-Manlius High School sports boosters raised $900,000 in a heartbeat to install a turf football field," while inner-city Fowler high "is forced to rely on charity for cleats for their football teams." Only three of the city's seventeen suburban school districts had even one school placed on the state's "need to improve" list, but so many city schools were cited that the whole district of Syracuse was placed on it for the eighth straight year. However, Syracuse's public schools made some advances with grants from the Say Yes to Education Foundation that provided extra tutoring and counseling and funds to enable poor children to attend college. In two years the number going to college with Say Yes help doubled from five hundred to nearly a thousand students. But there was no change in the city's high school graduation rate.[6]

Despite the success in Raleigh and other countywide school districts in the South, the outlook for achieving greater integration of schools by race or class is uncertain. The sweeping Republican victories in state legislatures and the United States Congress in the 2010 elections were seen by many as a rejection of "social engineering" imposed by liberal elites, an echo of the debate that led to the ouster of the Democrats in the Wake School Board election a year earlier.

Although the balance between liberty and equality has historically tipped toward liberty, there have been momentous shifts toward equality in the twentieth century—the passage of social security, the integration of the military, the GI bill, the Supreme Court's *Brown* decision ending segregated schools, the adoption of Medicare, and an expansion of civil rights. How that balance will be struck in Raleigh and the nation will define America in the twenty-first century.

November 16, 2010

Notes

Introduction

1. Kenneth T. Jackson, *Crabgrass Frontier: The Suburbanization of the United States* (New York: Oxford University Press, 1985).

1. What Happened to America's Cities?

1. Joyce Carol Oates, *What I Lived For* (New York: Plume-Penguin Books, 1995).
2. This paragraph and several that follow are drawn from Gerald Grant, "Fluctuations of Social Capital in an Urban Neighborhood," in Diane Ravitch and Joseph Viteritti, eds., *Making Good Citizens: Education and Civil Society* (New Haven: Yale University Press, 2001), pp. 96–121.
3. The center of the Westcott neighborhood lies on the line between two census tracts. The southern tract showed more moderate change, with an increase from nearly zero to 9 percent African American and a drop from 67 percent to 55 percent owner-occupied housing by 1970.
4. Jane Jacobs, *The Death and Life of Great American Cities* (New York: Vintage, 1961).
5. Kenneth T. Jackson, *Crabgrass Frontier: The Suburbanization of the United States* (New York: Oxford University Press, 1985), p. 208.
6. Ibid., p. 241.

7. Ibid., p. 214.

8. The study, by the National Training and Information Center of Chicago, analyzed FHA loans and default activity in 22 cities from 1996 to 2000, and was reported by Maureen Sieh in the Syracuse *Post-Standard,* May 21, 2002. A study of half a million mortgage applications in the Kansas City metropolitan area showed similar results: while minorities made up 19 percent of the population, they received less than 9 percent of the mortgage money lent in 1997. Ted Sickinger, "American Dream Denied," *The Kansas City Star,* February 28, 1999.

9. See http://www.metcoinc.org accessed December 11, 2008.

10. Susan E. Eaton, *The Other Boston Busing Story: What's Won and Lost across the Boundary Line* (New Haven: Yale University Press, 2001). Eaton interviewed a sample of 65 black adults who had attended METCO schools, 30 men and 35 women.

11. R. L. Zweigenhaft and G. W. Domhoff, *Blacks in the White Establishment: A Study of Race and Class in America* (New Haven: Yale University Press, 1991), cited in Eaton, *The Other Boston Busing Story,* pp. 235–236, 239.

12. William Julius Wilson, *When Work Disappears: The World of the New Urban Poor* (New York: Vintage, 1996). J. H. Braddock and J. M. McPartland, "How Minorities Continue to Be Excluded from Equal Employment Opportunities: Research on Labor Market and Institutional Barriers," *Journal of Social Issues* 43, no. 1 (1997): 5–39, cited in Eaton, *The Other Boston Busing Story,* p. 233.

13. Leonard Rubinowitz and James Rosenbaum, *Crossing Class and Color Lines: From Public Housing to White Suburbia* (Chicago: University of Chicago Press, 2000).

14. John Goering and Judith D. Feins, *Choosing a Better Life? Evaluating the Moving to Opportunity Social Experiment* (Washington, DC: The Urban Institute Press, 2003), p. 39.

15. Of $17 million in state aid for housing the poor and the elderly in central New York in 2008, slightly less than $1 million went to suburban areas for home repairs and housing for the elderly in suburban and rural areas. Most of the funds went for repair, refurbishing, and building low-income housing for the poor in Syracuse.

Delen Goldberg, "State Increases Housing Money," Syracuse *Post-Standard,* July 1, 2008.

16. Goering and Feins, *Choosing a Better Life,* p. 12.
17. Ibid., pp. 26–28, and Wilson, *When Work Disappears.*
18. Jackson, *Crabgrass Frontier,* pp. 149–151. The Morgan Park *Post* editorial is cited by Jackson on p. 151.
19. David Rusk, *Cities Without Suburbs* (Baltimore: Johns Hopkins University Press, 2003), p. 23.
20. Roscoe C. Martin, Frank J. Munger, et al., *Decisions in Syracuse: A Metropolitan Action Study* (New York: Anchor Books, 1965), pp. 219–234, 338.
21. Ibid., p. 103; Jackson, *Crabgrass Frontier,* pp. 138–149.
22. Paul A. Jargowsky, *Poverty and Place: Ghettos, Barrios and the American City* (New York: Russell Sage Foundation, 1997), p. viii. Jackson, *Crabgrass Frontier,* pp. 38, 62–63. For segregation indexes for 331 metropolitan areas, see the website at the Lewis Mumford Center for Comparative Urban and Regional Research at the State University of New York at Albany (http://mumford1.dyndns.org/cen2000/data.html).
23. Rusk, *Cities Without Suburbs,* p. xv. Here and in the following several pages my account condenses and occasionally paraphrases Rusk's inventive study.
24. Ibid, pp. 107–108.
25. Ibid., pp. 92–93.
26. Eric S. Belsky and Matthew Lambert, "Where Will They Live: Metropolitan Dimensions of Affordable Housing Problems," Joint Center for Housing Studies, Harvard University, September 2001 (http://www.jchs.harvard.edu/publications/communitydevelopment/belskylambert_w01-9.pdf).
27. David L. Kirp, John P. Dwyer, and Larry A. Rosenthal, *Our Town: Race, Housing and the Soul of Suburbia* (New Brunswick, NJ: 1997), p. 208. Rusk, *Cities Without Suburbs,* pp. 92–95.
28. Rusk, *Cities Without Suburbs,* pp. 96–97.
29. *Brown v. Board of Education,* 347 U.S. 483 (1954).
30. Roscoe C. Martin et al., *Decisions in Syracuse,* pp. 177–178.
31. *Milliken v. Bradley,* 418 U.S. 717 (1974).

2. Can This Neighborhood Be Saved?

1. Strictly speaking, James Hanley was not my uncle. He was the brother-in-law of my father's sister, but from childhood it was always "Uncle Jim and Aunt Rita" (Hanley).

2. This chapter draws on my essay, "Fluctuations of Social Capital in an Urban Neighborhood" that appeared in Diane Ravitch and Joseph P. Viteritti, eds., *Making Good Citizens: Education and Civil Society* (New Haven: Yale University Press, 2001). My research assistant, Jennifer Esposito, then a doctoral student at Syracuse University, conducted these interviews. Names have been disguised to ensure confidentiality.

3. Interview with Steve Susman, executive director of the Westcott Community Center, July 16, 2008.

4. Elijah Anderson, *Code of the Street: Decency, Violence, and the Moral Life of the Inner City* (New York: Norton, 1999).

5. "Hamilton High" is a pseudonym for a Syracuse high school. My original research agreement required that I disguise the name of this school.

6. Grant, *The World We Created at Hamilton High* (Cambridge: Harvard University Press, 1988), p. 35. The discussion here, for the purposes of illustrating the analysis of changes in social capital, necessarily collapses a complex account to be found in the first four chapters of *Hamilton High*.

7. Vanessa Siddle Walker, *Their Highest Potential: An African American School Community in the Segregated South* (Chapel Hill: University of North Carolina Press, 1996). Although she does not wish for a return to a segregated past, Walker's history of the Caswell County High School shows that it was a place of caring and high expectations, highly valued by its graduates. In *Getting Around Brown: Desegregation, Development, and the Columbus Public Schools* (Columbus: Ohio State University Press, 1998), Gregory S. Jacobs also discusses the loss of sympathetic and caring teaching suffered by many black students transferred to desegregated schools.

8. Donald Gates, *Potential Places of Informal Education within a Neighborhood Community,* unpublished paper, Syracuse University, 1997.

Ray Oldenburg referred to places of informal interaction as "third places," with the home being the "first place" and work sites being "second places." See Ray Oldenburg, *The Great Good Place* (New York: Norton, 1995). Gates, using city directories for relevant years, counted both work sites and informal gathering places.

9. Daniel Gonzalez, "Accusations Fly as Subsidy Cut: Syracuse Housing Authority Cites List of Neighborhood Complaints," Syracuse *Post-Standard*, June 10, 1999.

10. Christopher Jencks and Meredith Phillips, eds., *The Black-White Test Score Gap* (Washington, DC: Brookings Institute, 1998); Susan E. Mayer, *What Money Can't Buy: Family Income and Children's Life Chances* (Cambridge: Harvard University Press, 1997); William Julius Wilson, *When Work Disappears: The World of the New Urban Poor* (New York: Knopf, 1997).

11. Fred Siegel, *The Future Once Happened Here: New York, D.C., L.A., and the Fate of America's Big Cities* (New York: Free Press, 1997), p. 169.

12. Peter C. Baldwin, *Domesticating the Street: The Reform of Public Space in Hartford, 1850–1930* (Columbus: Ohio State University Press, 1999).

13. *The WENA News,* a publication of the Westcott East Neighborhood Association, "Small Miracles on Harvard Place," winter 1999–2000, p. 2.

3. Three Reconstructions of Raleigh

1. Elizabeth Reid Murray, *Wake: Capital County of North Carolina* (Raleigh: Capital County Publishing Co. 1983), p. 499.

2. Ibid., pp. 506–507.

3. William S. McFeeley, *Grant: A Biography* (New York: W. W. Norton Co., 1982), p. 227.

4. Murray, *Wake,* p. 527.

5. Eric Foner, *Forever Free: The Story of Emancipation and Reconstruction* (New York: Random House, 2006), pp. 3–6.

6. Murray, *Wake,* p. 579.

7. Ibid., pp. 553–554.

8. Mcfeeley, *Grant,* p. 259.

9. Foner, *Forever Free,* pp. 144–147.

10. Eric Anderson, *Race and Politics in North Carolina, 1872–1901: The Black Second* (Baton Rouge: Louisiana State University Press, 1981), p. x.

11. Nicholas Lemann, *Redemption: The Last Battle of the Civil War* (New York: Farrar, Straus, and Giroux, 2006), p. 150.

12. Murray, *Wake,* p. 596.

13. Anderson, *Race and Politics,* pp. 227, 266.

14. Foner, *Forever Free,* pp. 160–61. Anderson, p. 250.

15. Anderson, *Race and Politics,* p. 264.

16. Ibid., pp. 36–37, 62–63, 168–169, 207, 294–295.

17. Ibid., pp. 16–17, 22–24.

18. Ibid., pp. 4–5.

19. Foner, *Forever Free,* pp. 194, 214. Wilmoth A Carter, *The Urban Negro in the South* (New York: Vantage Press, 1962), p. 88.

20. Anderson, *Race and Politics,* pp. 296–97.

21. C. Vann Woodward, *The Strange Career of Jim Crow* (New York: Oxford Press, 2001), pp. 80–81.

22. Anderson, *Race and Politics,* p. 308. Carter, *Urban Negro in the South,* pp. 88–89.

23. C. Vann Woodward, *Origins of the New South, 1877–1913* (Baton Rouge: Louisiana State University Press, 1951), p. 357. Foner, *Forever Free,* p. 212.

24. Raleigh *News and Observer,* November 1, 1936, quoted in Jack Michael McElreath, *The Cost of Opportunity: School Desegregation and Changing Racial Relations in the Triangle since World War II,* Ph.D. diss, University of Pennsylvania, 2002, chap. 2.

25. Raleigh *News and Observer,* November 2, 1936, quoted in McElreath, *The Cost of Opportunity,* chap. 1.

26. Carter, *Urban Negro in the South,* pp. 95–96.

27. McElreath, *The Cost of Opportunity,* chaps. 3 and 4.

28. Ibid., chap. 5.

29. John Patrick Daly, *When Slavery Was Called Freedom: Evangelicalism, Proslavery, and the Causes of the Civil War* (Lexington: University Press of Kentucky, 2002), p. 144.

30. McElreath, *The Cost of Opportunity*, chap. 5.

31. Ibid., chap. 7.

32. Ibid., chap. 8.

33. Gene Marlow, "Report Says Merge Schools Here," Raleigh *News and Observer*, April 25, 1965.

34. "Not the Last Step," Raleigh *News and Observer*, April 24, 1968.

35. Raleigh *News and Observer*, August 10, 1971.

36. Author interview with Paul Jervay, January 27, 2003.

37. McElreath, *The Cost of Opportunity*, chap. 9.

38. Author interview with Vernon Malone, February 27, 2003.

4. There Are No Bad Schools in Raleigh

1. These are 2003 scores. By 2006, Syracuse had fallen to 21 percent passing.

2. In this chapter and hereafter, in referring to the merged Raleigh–Wake County school system, I use Raleigh and Wake County schools interchangeably.

3. All quotations in this chapter are drawn from interviews by the author, except where noted otherwise.

4. See Richard Kahlenberg, *All Together Now: Creating Middle Class Schools through Public School Choice* (Washington, DC: Brookings Institution Press, 2003), and Allan Ornstein, *Class Counts: Education, Inequality, and the Shrinking Middle Class* (New York: Rowman and Littlefield, 2007).

5. Susan Leigh Flinspach and Karen E. Banks, "Moving Beyond Race: Socioeconomic Diversity as a Race-Neutral Approach to Desegregation in the Wake County Schools," in John Charles Boger and Gary Orfield, eds., *School Resegregation: Must the South Turn Back?* (Chapel Hill: University of North Carolina Press, 2005).

6. North Carolina State Department of Education, 2006 Adequate Yearly Progress Report, Results by Subgroup.

7. I thank one of the anonymous reviewers of this manuscript for suggesting this typology.

8. National Commission on Teaching and America's Future, *What Matters Most: Teaching for America's Future* (New York, 1996).

9. On the value of reforming grade schools first, see E. D. Hirsch, "An Epoch-Making Report, But What About the Early Grades," *Education Week*, April 23, 2008.

10. See Ronald F. Ferguson, *Excellence with Equity: An Emerging Vision for Closing the Achievement Gap* (Cambridge: Harvard Education Press, 2007), and Richard F. Elmore, "The Limits of Change," *Harvard Education Letter*, January 2002.

11. David Armor is among those who have said one of the shortcomings of most reforms introduced in the wake of the No Child Left Behind law is that advocates assumed they could close the achievement gap without any changes in families. Wake County did not assume that. See Armor's "No Excuses: Simplistic Solution for the Achievement Gap?" *Teachers College Record*, February 12, 2004. On the value of expanding time for instruction, see Tommy M. Tomlinson, ed., *Motivating Students to Learn: Overcoming Barriers to High Achievement* (Berkeley: McCutchan Publishing, 1993), and Susan H. Fuhrman, "If We're Talking About Race, Let's Talk About Education," *Education Week*, May 7, 2008.

12. T. Keung Hui, "Voters Leaning Against Wake School Bond Issue," Raleigh *News and Observer*, October 25, 2006.

13. T. Keung Hui, "Cary, Central Raleigh Key to Bond Vote," Raleigh *News and Observer*, November 9, 2006.

14. Todd Silberman, "Wake Schools Find Diversity Hard to Sustain," Raleigh *News and Observer*, June 11, 2006.

15. Scores for 2008 were not available as this book went to press.

16. Bill McNeal and Tom Oxholm, *A School District's Journey to Excellence* (Thousand Oaks, CA: Corwin Press, 2008), p. 69.

17. Ibid. See also T. Keung Hui, "Is Diversity Worth the Effort?" Raleigh *News and Observer*, October 30, 2005.

5. A Tragic Decision

1. In a 1992 Detroit survey, 53 percent of whites said they would not feel comfortable living in a racially integrated neighborhood. See Reynolds Farley, Sheldon Danziger, and Harry J. Holzer, *Detroit Divided* (New York: Russell Sage Foundation, 2000), pp. 196–201.

2. Rick Moriarty and Terri Weaver, "How New York Lost Control of

Tax Breaks for Businesses," Syracuse *Post-Standard,* September 21, 2003. Peter Lyman, "Syracuse Short on Job Results for Tax Incentives," Syracuse *Post-Standard,* December 13, 2004.

3. Frederic Pierce, "Big Dreams for Oil City Failed to Come True," Syracuse *Post-Standard,* May 21, 2000. Construction began in 2007 on a conventional addition to the mall: Rick Moriarty, "Destiny to Hold Summits on Construction," Syracuse *Post-Standard,* September 7, 2007.

4. Marnie Eisenstadt and Greg Munno, "The Man Buying Syracuse," Syracuse *Post-Standard,* March 13, 2005. Charley Hannagan, "Hotel Syracuse Sits Silent and Empty," Syracuse *Post-Standard,* May 29, 2004. Three years later an attempt was being made to revive the hotel. Rick Moriarty, "Excellus Gives Up on City: 850 Jobs Head to DeWitt," Syracuse *Post-Standard,* July 24, 2007. "The Heart of CNY: Report Makes It Clear: What's Good for Downtown Is Good for the Region," Syracuse *Post-Standard,* editorial, May 13, 2007.

5. Nancy Buczek, "Grant to Help Link 3 Universities," Syracuse *Post-Standard,* February 25, 2006. Syracuse did have some other science links with area universities, however.

6. Jennifer S. Vey, *Restoring Prosperity: The State Role in Revitalizing America's Older Industrial Cities* (Washington, DC: Brookings Institution, 2007), pp. 74–75.

7. "Syracuse Is the Shining Light," published by the Matthew J. Driscoll for Mayor Committee, no date.

8. In Philadelphia, for example, only 1 percent of the city's public school teachers earned more than $70,000 a year in 2003, whereas a quarter to half of the teachers in Philadelphia's suburbs earned more than that. See Ruth Curran Neild, Elizabeth Useem, Eva F. Travers, and Joy Lesnick, "Once and For All: Placing a Highly Qualified Teacher in Every Philadelphia Classroom," published by Research for Action, Philadelphia, 2003.

9. Heather Rose, Jon Sonstelie, Ray Reinhard, and Sharmaine Heng, "High Expectations, Modest Means: The Challenge Facing California's Public Schools," published by The Public Policy Institute of California, October 2003.

10. Under a grant from the Say Yes Foundation, the Syracuse school

district planned to provide more counseling, after-school tutoring and mentoring, and full-day pre-kindergarten programs. Syracuse University and twenty-four other private colleges have pledged free tuition and books to any low-income city child who qualifies for admission, beginning with the entering class of 2009. If the New York State legislature approves, it would also assure free tuition at all state colleges.

11. *Green v. County School Board of New Kent County,* 391 U.S. 430 (1968).
12. The Charlotte plan was upheld in *Swann v. Charlotte-Mecklenburg Board of Education,* 402 U.S. 1 (1971). This analysis also draws on John C. Jeffries Jr., *Justice Lewis F. Powell, Jr.: A Biography* (New York: Fordham University Press, 2001).
13. *Keyes v. School District No. 1, Denver, Colorado,* 413 U.S. 189 (1973).
14. Farley, Danziger, and Holzer, *Detroit Divided.*
15. Eleanor P. Wolf, *Trial and Error: The Detroit School Segregation Case* (Detroit: Wayne State University Press, 1981), p. 18.
16. *Bradley v. Milliken.* 1971. Civ. Action 35257. E. D. Michigan.
17. Farley, Danziger, and Holzer, *Detroit Divided,* pp. 40–41.
18. Warren Weaver, "U.S. Opposes Detroit Integration Plan," *New York Times,* February 28, 1974, and the Associated Press, "Court to Rehear Detroit Bus Plan," *New York Times,* January 17, 1973.
19. *Milliken v. Bradley,* 418 U.S. 717 (1974).
20. Ibid.
21. See Jeffries, *Lewis F. Powell, Jr.;* John W. Dean, *The Rehnquist Choice* (New York: Simon and Schuster, 2001); and Bob Woodward and Scott Armstrong, *The Brethren: Inside the Supreme Court* (New York: Simon and Schuster, 1979).
22. Dean, *The Rehnquist Choice,* pp. 46–51, 102.
23. *Keyes v. School District No. 1, Denver, Colorado,* 413 U.S. 189 (1973).
24. Jeffries, *Lewis F. Powell, Jr.,* p. 303.
25. Richard L. Madden, "Nixon Gets Education Bill with Busing Restrictions," *New York Times,* August 1, 1974; Jack Rosenthal, "'Hypocrisy' on Desegregation Charged," *New York Times,* September 23, 1970.

26. Howard Schuman, Charlotte Steeh, Lawrence Bobo, and Maria Krysan, *Racial Attitudes in America* (Cambridge: Harvard University Press, 1997), p. 104.
27. Ibid., p. 126.
28. Ibid., pp. 123, 248.
29. Walter Rugaber, "Wallace Sweeps Primary in Michigan and Wins Handily in Maryland," *New York Times,* May 17, 1972.
30. Richard L. Madden, "Senate Liberals Fail to Shut Off Debate on a Measure That Would Curb Busing," *New York Times,* September 24, 1975.
31. Abraham Ribicoff, *Congressional Record, Senate* 118:3579, February 24, 1972, cited in Jeffries, *Lewis F. Powell, Jr.,* p. 302.
32. Jeffries, *Lewis F. Powell, Jr.,* p. 302.

6. What Should We Hope For?

1. *Regents of the University of California v. Bakke,* 438 U.S. 265 (1978).
2. This was true in the most diverse schools. For example, at Bugg Elementary School, where 56 percent of the children are black and a quarter of all children are poor enough to qualify for subsidized lunches, 98 percent of parents said "My child's school is a safe place to learn" and 94 percent of students agreed. Eighty-eight percent of parents affirmed that "students at my child's school are well behaved overall." Wake County Public Schools, Evaluation and Research Department, Parents' Surveys, 2003 and 2006.
3. James Coleman et al., *Equality of Educational Opportunity* (Washington, DC: Government Printing Office, 1966).
4. Gerald Grant, "Shaping Social Policy: The Politics of the Coleman Report," *Teachers College Record,* Fall 1973.
5. Coleman, *Equality of Educational Opportunity,* p. 325.
6. Judith R. Smith, Jeanne Brooks-Gunn, and Pamela K. Klebanov, "Consequences of Living in Poverty for Young Children's Cognitive and Verbal Ability and Early School Achievement," in Greg J. Duncan and Jeanne Brooks-Gunn, eds., *Consequences of Growing Up Poor* (New York: Russell Sage Foundation, 1997), pp. 132–189.
7. The Gates-funded report says there has been little success in turnaround efforts on a large scale. It believes it could happen by in-

creasing funding up to a million dollars per school per year and creating special "turnaround zones" with specially trained staffs in inner-city schools. Such efforts should certainly be tried. But Coleman's research and other studies cited here raise the question whether any "zone" that does not include middle-class children is likely to succeed in the long run. See William Calkins et al., "The Turnaround Challenge," Mass Insight Education and Research Institute, Boston, 2007. See Abigail Thernstrom and Stephen Thernstrom, *No Excuses: Closing the Racial Gap in Learning* (New York: Simon and Schuster, 2003), for an argument in favor of the KIPP reforms. For an expansion of the view advocated here, see Richard Rothstein, *Class and Schools* (New York: Teachers College Press, 2004), pp. 61–84, and Richard D. Kahlenberg, *All Together Now: Creating Middle-Class Schools through Public School Choice* (Washington, DC: Brookings Institution Press, 2001).

8. Andy Smarick, "Wave of the Future: Why Charter Schools Should Replace Failing Urban Schools," *Education Next* 8, no. 1 (Winter 2008): 38–45. The Washington test data was from the 2005 National Assessment of Educational Progress test.

9. Gary Orfield and Chungmei Lee, "Why Segregation Matters: Poverty and Educational Inequality," The Civil Rights Project at the University of California, Los Angeles, January 2005.

10. Roslyn Arlin Mickelson, "The Incomplete Desegregation of the Charlotte-Mecklenburg Schools and Its Consequences," in John Charles Boger and Gary Orfield, eds., *School Resegregation: Must the South Turn Back?* (Chapel Hill: University of North Carolina Press, 2005), p. 93.

11. Ann Bradley, "Tennessee Waltz," *Education Week,* October 1, 1995. Beth Reinhard, "Us Versus Them? Chattanooga Prepares for Merger," *Education Week,* June 18, 1997. Bess Keller, "Merger Makes a Difference," *Education Week,* March 1, 2006. Hamilton County Department of Education, "Hamilton County Schools Continue to Improve Performance on State Report Card: Overall Achievement Scores Rise 7 years Running," November 2, 2007.

12. Orfield and Lee, "Why Segregation Matters."

13. Michael Kurlaender and John T. Yun, "Is Diversity a Compelling

Educational Interest? Evidence from Louisville," in Gary Orfield and Michael Kurlaender, eds., *Diversity Challenged: Evidence on the Impact of Affirmative Action* (Cambridge: Harvard Education Publishing Group, 2001), p. 117.

14. *Meredith v. Jefferson County Board of Education,* June 28, 2007. The Fairfax policy has been challenged by parents who claim the School Board exceeded its authority by taking socioeconomic factors into account when redrawing attendance zones. See Angela Ciolfi and James E. Ryan, "Socioeconomic Integration: It's Legal and It Makes Sense," *Education Week,* June 18, 2008.

15. Russell W. Rumberger and Gregory J. Palardy, "Does Segregation Still Matter? The Impact of Student Composition on Academic Achievement in High School," *Teachers College Record* 107, no. 9 (2005).

16. William Julius Wilson, *The Declining Significance of Race: Blacks and Changing American Institutions* (Chicago: University of Chicago Press, 1980), and *The Truly Disadvantaged: The Inner City, the Underclass, and Public Policy* (Chicago: University of Chicago Press, 1993).

17. Pedro Carneiro and James J. Heckman, "Human Capital Policy," paper presented at the Alvin Hansen Seminar, Harvard University, April 2002, cited in Richard Rothstein, *Class and Schools* (New York: Teachers College Press, 2004), pp. 99–102.

18. Todd Silberman, "Diversity in Schools," Raleigh *News and Observer,* January 23, 2000, and Silberman, "New Plan, Old Issues," Raleigh *News and Observer,* January 22, 2000.

19. Joyce L. Epstein, "After the Bus Arrives: Resegregation in Desegregated Schools," *Journal of Social Issues* 41, no. 3 (1985): 23–43. See also Jeannie Oakes, "Tracking in Secondary Schools: A Contextual Perspective," *Educational Psychologist* 22, no. 2 (1987): 129–153.

20. Interview with Tom Oxholm, April 4, 2004.

21. Howard Schuman, Charlotte Stech, Laurence Bobo, and Maria Krysan, *Racial Attitudes in America* (Cambridge: Harvard University Press, 1997), pp. 140–141. Steve Farkas and Jean Johnson, *Time to Move On: African-American and White Parents Set an Agenda for Public Schools* (New York: Public Agenda, 1998), p. 41.

22. North Carolina received a grade of B+ and New York an A on a comparison of state standards, assessments, and accountability. See "Quality Counts," Editorial Projects in Education Research Center, Washington, D.C., January 2008.

23. Department of Evaluation and Research, Wake County Public Schools.

24. Christopher Jencks, *Who Gets Ahead? The Determinants of Economic Success in America* (New York: Basic Books, 1979).

25. Scott E. Page, *The Difference: How the Power of Diversity Creates Better Groups, Firms, Schools, and Societies* (Princeton: Princeton University Press, 2007), pp. 9–10. See also Claudia Dreifus, "In Professor's Model, Diversity = Productivity," *New York Times*, January 8, 2008.

26. Susan E. Eaton, *The Other Boston Busing Story: What's Won and Lost across the Boundary Line* (New Haven: Yale University Press, 2001). Amy Stuart Wells and Robert L. Crain, *Stepping Over the Color Line* (New Haven: Yale University Press, 1997). Wells, "Re-examining Social Science Research on School Desegregation," *Teachers College Record* 96 (Summer): 691–706. Christopher G. Ellison and Daniel A. Powers, "The Contact Hypothesis and Racial Attitudes among Black Americans," *Social Science Quarterly* 75 (June 1994): 385–400. Robert L. Crain et al., *Making Desegregation Work: How Schools Create Social Climates* (Washington, DC: Rand Corporation, 1982). Also, Janet Ward Schofield, "Review of Research on School Desegregation's Impact on Elementary and Secondary School Students," in James A. Banks and Cherry A. McGee Banks, eds., *Handbook of Research on Multicultural Education* (New York: Macmillan Publishing, 1995), pp. 597–616.

27. Leonard S. Rubinowitz and James E. Rosenbaum, *Class and Color Lines: From Public Housing to White Suburbia* (Chicago: University of Chicago Press, 2000).

28. See Charles C. Moskos and John Sibley Butler, *All That We Can Be: Black Leadership and Racial Integration the Army Way* (New York: Basic Books, 1993), esp. chapter 5, "Preparing Soldiers for a Level Playing Field."

29. Jennifer S. Vey, *Restoring Prosperity: The State Role in Revitalizing*

America's Older Industrial Cities (Washington, DC: Brookings Institution, 2007), pp. 20, 26.

30. Ron Wolk, "Flight from Failure," *Teacher Magazine* 50, no. 3 (December 2006).

31. Debra Viadero, "No Quick Fixes to 'Poverty Gap' under NCLB," *Education Week*, November 8, 2007. See also Adam Gamoran, ed., *Standards-Based Reform and the Poverty Gap* (Washington, DC: Brookings Institution Press, 2007).

32. Andrew Calkins et al., *The Turnaround Challenge*, p. 5.

33. Diana Jean Schemo, "Failing Schools Strain to Meet U.S. Standard," *New York Times*, October 16, 2007.

34. "School Districts Start to Face Sanctions under Landmark Law," *Education Week*, May 12, 2008.

35. Susan Eaton, *The Other Boston Busing Story*. See also the METCO program website: www.doe.mass.edu/metco.

36. Gerald Grant, *The World We Created at Hamilton High* (Cambridge: Harvard University Press, 1988).

37. Demographic data for 2006 from the New York State Department of Education.

38. *Dorset County Chronicle*, May 22, 1834. Cited in Claire Tomalin, *Thomas Hardy* (New York: Penguin Press, 2007) p. 36.

Epilogue

1. Letter from Karen Nelson, "The People's Forum," Raleigh *News and Observer*, January 16, 2008.

2. Letters from Ashley Bertz, Raleigh *News and Observer*, January 16, 2008, and Marc Landry, January 27, 2008. Rosa Gill's comments were reported by Meiling Arounnarath, "Dozens Rally in Cary against Reassignments," Raleigh *News and Observer*, January 13, 2008.

3. T. Keung Hui, "Wake Parents Sour on Reassignments," Raleigh *News and Observer*, January 9, 2008.

4. Cindy Schaefer, "Greater Expectations for All Students," Raleigh *News and Observer*, January 18, 2008, and Karen Campbell, "It's a County System," January 27, 2008.

5. Kinea White Epps, "Wake Schools Delay Diversity Policy," Raleigh *News and Observer,* October 10, 2007.

6. In 2007, a family of four qualified for federally subsidized lunches if they earned less than $38,203 a year. Wake's high school dropout rate rose from 3.88 percent in 2006 to 4.21 percent in 2007, still significantly lower than the statewide average of 5.24 percent. T. Keung Hui, "Dropout Rate, Suspensions on Rise in North Carolina," Raleigh *News and Observer,* February 8, 2008.

7. The data for Raleigh students reflect 2007 scores on North Carolina state tests, for Syracuse students 2008 scores on New York state tests. Math scores in Raleigh also reflected stiffer statewide tests adopted in 2005, and renormed reading tests were expected to depress scores in 2008.

8. Chris Giattina, Ken Bowers, Anindita Mitra, Deana Swetlik, and Erin Simmons, "Syracuse: Communities Making Connections at the Crossroads of Upstate New York: A Sustainable Design Assessment Team Report," American Institute of Architects Center for Communities by Design, December 2006, p. 3.

Postscript

1. T. Keung Hui and Thomas Goldsmith, "Citing Conscience, Wake Schools Chief Resigns," Raleigh *News and Observer,* February 17, 2010. Anne Blythe and Thomas Goldsmith, "Hundreds Rally against Wake Schools Plan," *News and Observer,* July 20, 2010.

2. T. Keung Hui, "Wake Schools Give No Data to Accrediting Agency," *News and Observer,* October 2, 2010. T. Keung Hui, Thomas Goldsmith, and Mandy Locke, "NAACP Takes Wake to Feds," *News and Observer,* September 26, 2010. Thomas Goldsmith and T. Keung Hui, "Wake Leaders Strike Back on Schools," *News and Observer,* September 17, 2010.

3. Miranda Miller, letter to the editor, *News and Observer,* October 8, 2010.

4. T. Keung Hui, "Tedesco Feels RWCA's Wrath," *News and Observer,* September 17, 2010. T. Keung Hui, "Wake Teachers Give School Board Low Marks," *News and Observer,* October 15, 2010.

5. Thomas Goldsmith and T. Keung Hui, "Wake Schools Toss Out Zone Assignment Plan," *News and Observer,* October 6, 2010. Thomas Goldsmith, "Wake's School Board Move Will Delay Big Changes," *News and Observer,* October 7, 2010.

6. Thomas Buckel, "How to Control Spending in Onondaga County," Syracuse *Post-Standard,* September 12, 2010. Ed Griffin-Nolan, "Best Urban-Suburban Disconnect," Syracuse *New Times,* September 29, 2010. Maureen Nolan and Catie O'Toole, "NY Passes 4, Demotes 4 on 'In Need' Listing," Syracuse *Post-Standard,* November 5, 2010.

Acknowledgments

Most good books can be traced to a few fundamental ideas. This book is rooted in friendships with three extraordinary men going back to my days as a graduate student: James Coleman, Nathan Glazer, and Daniel Patrick Moynihan. I owe my greatest intellectual debt to James Coleman, whom I met when his landmark study linking social capital to equal educational opportunity was published in 1966. A frustrated chemist who rose to be a giant of sociology at Johns Hopkins University and later at the University of Chicago, Coleman became a generous tutor in meetings and through correspondence when I decided to write my dissertation on "The Politics of the Coleman Report."

Nathan Glazer transformed my knowledge of the links between education and social policy when I served as his teaching assistant in a course on urban social policy at Harvard University. Although Glazer might not agree with the policy conclusions I have drawn here, I could not have made them without understanding how social policies shape schools. School reformers too often fail to see those connections and talk as if "break-the-mold" schools can be concocted in a laboratory and planted in freshly furrowed ground like new genetic strains of corn.

Daniel Patrick Moynihan, then director of the Joint Center for Urban Studies at Harvard and MIT, was also an early mentor who convinced me to undertake a doctorate. While he spent most of his academic career at Harvard, he began it as a young assistant professor at Syracuse University, where he wrote a book about Governor Averill Harriman.

He came back to spend his final years as University Professor at Syracuse, and at our dinner table one night he critiqued an essay that was the germ of this book—his opinions interspersed with choice bits of personal history and long quotations from William Butler Yeats. This engaging conversation was typical of the wisdom and passion Moynihan brought to any discussion of politics.

I wish I had been able to help my graduate students as much as they have helped me. In particular, those who served as research assistants gave unstintingly—not only in combing through research libraries and doing interviews but also providing the intellectual friction that gave this book more traction. First among these were Jennifer Esposito, Donald Gates, Jane Greiner, and April Harris, supported by the Hannah Hammond Fund (Hammond endowed one of the first professorships at Syracuse University). Next were those who worked on The Educational Life of a Metropolitan Community, a research project sponsored by the Spencer Foundation: Lorraine Bedy, Zoltan Bedy, Ronnie Casella, Kelley Greenman Crouse, Neil Funk-Unrau, Don Haviland, Redell Hearn, Denise Johnson, John Randall, Karen Stearns, and Frank T. Zsigo.

In addition to the support from the Hannah Hammond Fund and the Spencer Foundation, let me express gratitude for a year spent at the Center for Advanced Study in the Behavioral Sciences at Stanford University, where I first began to formulate the ideas that led to this book. Conversations there with John Baugh, Lawrence Bobo, Linda Marie Burton, Shirley Brice Heath, Qicheng Jing, Christopher Lasch, Robert S. Lawrence, Nell Irvin Painter, Robert Putnam, Barbara Rogoff, Robert Rosenthal, Ian Shapiro, and Robert S. Weiss were invaluable.

I have been blessed by extraordinary colleagues at Syracuse University who both challenged and inspired me: Barbara Applebaum, Douglas Biklen, Sari Knopp Biklen, Bob Bogdan, John Briggs, Joan Burstyn, Robert Daly, Thomas Green, Ralph Ketcham, Emily Robertson, Manfred Stanley, and Kenneth Strike. Many of my students became colleagues as well, particularly those in my seminar "Can Urban Schools Be Saved?"

I taught high school students in both Syracuse and Raleigh, whose essays about life in their own school provided valuable insights for this book. In Syracuse, special mention should be made of Keenan Adenau,

Eric Altman, Robbie Cary, Naomi Ciaramella, Mike DeBoer, Julie Emm, Ben Metzler, Elias Musallam, Ashleigh Tubb, Naike Wewer, and their regular social studies teacher, Nick Stamoulacatos. In Raleigh, Twan Morris, Tere Peterson, Amy Riggleman, Nathan Sherrill, and Maurice Spearsand deserve to be singled out, along with their English teacher Barbara Nichols.

Special thanks go to colleagues at North Carolina State University in Raleigh, where I spent three semesters as a visiting research professor, one of them at the William Friday Institute. Kay Moore, dean of the School of Education, along with Paul Bitting, Carol Kasworm, Robert Serow, and Hiller Spires, helped this Yankee make all the right contacts and saved me from taking many wrong turns. Peter Hessling pointed me toward historical sources, and the sociologist Donald Tomaskovic-Devey was most helpful in the early stages of my research, as were John Dye and George Noblit at the University of North Carolina at Chapel Hill, and Stanley J. Elliott at St. Augustine College.

Karen Allen, director of the Olivia Raney Library in Raleigh, opened special historical collections for me there. Steve Massengill was of great assistance at the North Carolina State Archives, as was Todd Johnson at the Raney Library, who was at work on the second volume of a history of Raleigh. Jack Michael McElreath was most generous in sharing a draft of his dissertation on desegregation in the Research Triangle. In Syracuse, Dennis J. Connors, curator of history at the Onondaga Historical Association, was a helpful guide to collections there, as was Dianne Hagan at the Carrier Air Conditioning Company archives.

Of many who helped me understand the wider political and social context of Raleigh, my first thanks go to former Governor James Hunt. Ralph Campbell Jr., then state auditor, also opened many doors. Vernon Malone, who had been chair of the merged Wake County School Board, then county commissioner and a member of the State Legislature, provided a rich political and social history of Raleigh. State legislators J. Allen Adams, Bernard Allen, and Paul Luebke also offered many insights. Others who agreed to sit for interviews included Kenneth Bowers, assistant director of city planning for Raleigh; Yvonne Brannon, former county commissioner and director of the Center for Urban Affairs at North Carolina State University; George Chapman, former director of planning for Raleigh; Frank A. Daniels Jr., former publisher of the Raleigh *News and Observer;* Lucy Daniels, author; Paul Jervay, publisher of *The Carolinian;* Harrison Marshall, former planner for the North Carolina Department of Transportation; Cynthia Matson, president of Assignment By Choice; Charles Meeker, current mayor of Raleigh; Sharon Rene Peterson of the Wake County Planning Department; Prezelle Robinson, former president of St. Augustine College; Jennifer Song of the Wake County Planning Department; and Smedes York, former mayor of Raleigh.

In research over seven years, I visited nearly a score of schools, observed dozens of classes, and had access to all levels of the Wake County school system. I am most grateful for interviews with former school superintendents Bill McNeal and Bob Bridges and current superintendent Del Burns. I want to express my appreciation to former School Board members John Gilbert, Tom Oxholm, and Susan Parry; former associate superintendents Walt Sherlin and Robert T. Williams; director of magnet programs Caroline Massengill; former director of evaluation Karen Banks, and her successor, David Holdzkom; attorney for Wake County schools Ann Majestic; president of the Wake County Educational Partnership Tony Habit; the North Carolina Forum on Public Education's president, John N. Dornan, and its director of policy research, John Poteat; and president of the Wake County branch of the North Carolina Education Association Charlotte Turpin.

Some of the most talented people I have met are principals and teachers in Wake's schools. Among the principals I was fortunate to interview at length were David Ansbacher, Beth Cochran, William Crockett, Dana King, John Modest, Edye Morris-Bryant, Brandy Nelson, Mary Page, Diane Payne, Jane Slay, Alynna Stone, and Roy Teel. Among the teachers: Loren Baron, Shakira Chandra, Chris Danehower, Margo Dawson, Shari Frederick, Robert Grant, Lexa Kaplan, Jan Kidwell, Cora McMillan, Chris Newton, Barbara Nichols, Leigh Noonan, Jo Ann Norris, Helen Roberts, Martin Rudd, Catherine Rush, James Shaw, Meredith Solesz, and Che Von Stone. Parents and alumni of Wake schools interviewed included John T. Atkins, Marge Bailey, Susan Bridges, Angela Baker Cloud, Wiley M. Davis, Pamela DeLoatch, Darcenia Hammond, Joseph Holt Jr., Leonard Hunter, and Lisa Mial.

This book draws on earlier research in Syracuse acknowledged in *The World We Created at Hamilton High*. For the present work, in addition to those noted above, I am grateful for interviews granted to me or to my research assistants with Robert Doucette, developer of Syracuse's Armory Square District; Robert Haley, architect; Stephen Jones, former school superintendent; Karen Kitney, director of the Syracuse–Onondaga County Planning Commission; John F. Mahoney, former assistant to Congressman James Hanley; Joseph Mareane, chief fiscal officer of Onondaga County; Lorraine Merrick, deputy superintendent; Ann Michel, former assistant to Mayor Lee Alexander and president of Knowledge Systems Research; John Patterson, teacher, actor, and former classmate at Syracuse Central High; Vito Sciscioli, whose portfolio includes many civic and political roles; Tom Young, former mayor.

Also, Cynthia Carrington, former executive director of the Westcott Community Development Corporation; Eloise Dowdell Curry, president of the Urban League of Onondaga County; James Dessauer, director of Eastside Neighbors In Progress; Jesse Dowdell, director of the Southwest Community Center; Clarence C. Dunham, who served ten terms on the Onondaga County Legislature; Rufus Hills a member of the Westcott East Neighborhood Association; Tracy Hogarth, program director of Girls Inc.; Vanessa Johnson of the Onondaga Historical Association; Deborah Mastropaolo, principal of Nottingham High School; Jackie Warren Moore, a poet who also teaches in Syracuse area prisons; William Moran, executive director of the Hiawatha Council Boy Scouts; Minister Mark Muhammad; Steve Susman, executive director of the Westcott Community Center; Hope Wallis, director of American Friends Service Committee; Brian Walton, president of the board of Catholic Charities; Hal Welsh, director of the Onondaga County YMCA; and Heather Wyncoop, program director of American Friends Service Committee. I am also indebted to several senior citizens who talked with my team about growing up in inner-city Syracuse: Cornelia Adams, Barbara Cole, Eloise Curry, and Alan Green. Yale University Press kindly permitted me to include revised segments of my essay "Fluctuations of Social Capital in an Urban Neighborhood" in what eventually became Chapter 2 of this volume.

My editor at Harvard University Press, Michael Aronson, never lost patience as research dragged on, postponing deadline after deadline; on the contrary, he called with encouraging words. I was blessed by an unusually gifted editor of the manuscript, Susan Wallace Boehmer. Few pages of this book were not improved by her labors. My wife, Judith Dunn Grant, contributed some of the best interviews of parents and alumni of Raleigh schools and brought an unerring eye to her critique of early drafts of the manuscript.

Index

Index

Index